The Monster With A Thousand Faces

The Monster With A Thousand Faces:

Guises of the Vampire in Myth and Literature

by

Brian J. Frost

Bowling Green State University Popular Press
Bowling Green, Ohio 43403

Library of Congress Catalogue Card No.: 89-061747

ISBN: 0-87972-459-5 Clothbound
       0-87972-460-9 Paperback

Cover design by Greg Budgett and Gary Dumm

Dedicated to Frank H. Parnell,
in gratitude for his help and encouragement.

Contents

There are vampires and vampires,
and not all of them suck blood.

Fritz Leiber

Foreword

Ever since Hollywood cashed in on the box-office potential of Bram Stoker's immortal *Dracula,* and turned the human bloodsucker into a stereotype, the popular image of the vampire has been that of a suave, fang-toothed nobleman in black evening dress and opera cloak, who goes around sucking the blood of nubile young women. Unfortunately, this has tended to obscure the fact that the vampire is a polymorphic phenomenon with a host of disparate guises to its credit, some of which are by no means fictional. Therefore, in the first part of this book, I have attempted to set the record straight by providing the reader with a comprehensive inventory of the vampire's guises in fact and fiction, and have also tried to offer some explanation for the vampire's continuing hold on our imaginations.

Perhaps the most remarkable characteristic of the vampire is its ability to adapt to changing social and environmental conditions. Ever moving with the times, it has evolved over untold centuries from obscure beginnings—probably as some hideous monstrosity—to its present-day embodiment as a psychopathic killer with a blood fixation. And yet, despite its many faces, this multi-monster has remained basically the same—a destructive, self-seeking force. Another link between all the different vampire species—the common denominator, if you like—is the exclusivity of their diet. For no matter what form they take, all vampires obtain their sustenance in the same way—by absorbing or ingesting the vital essences of living organisms.

Man's attitude toward the vampire, particularly the human species popularly known as the Undead, has always been somewhat contradictory—a mixture of revulsion and fascination. This ambivalence probably arises from the fact that our natural abhorrence of such anomalies is tinged with a sneaking admiration for their ability to cheat death, disgusted though we are by the means employed. However, let those who scoff at the notion of vampires remember that there have

1

been, and always will be, desperate people who will pay *any* price for immortality. As the famous quote preceding Poe's "Ligeia" asserts: "Man doth not yield himself to the angels, nor unto death utterly, save only through the weakness of his feeble will". This being so, the first requirement of any would-be vampire is an indomitable will to survive. Given that kind of momentum, surely almost anything—metamorphosis into a vampire included—might be possible.

The second part of this book is a historical survey of the vampire story, showing how the fictional image of the vampire has also changed over the years. Although a lot of ground is covered—more than in any other comparable work—I do not want to leave anyone with the impression that this is in any way an exhaustive survey. In fact, I have merely scraped the surface, and there can be little doubt that the several hundred works of fiction mentioned herein are only the tip of the iceberg. However, if what I have been able to unearth encourages you to seek out some of the rarer items and sample their delights, I will consider all my long hours of research worthwhile.

As this book amply demonstrates, the vampire story has, in the past, been enormously popular with authors and readers alike, and the signs are that its future will be just as rosy. Indeed, the number of vampire novels published in the United States and Britain in recent years has been truly phenomenal, and there seems every likelihood that the subject of vampirism, in all its fantastic forms, will continue to be a major source of inspiration for writers of weird fiction for many years to come.

Finally, thanks are offered to the following for their generous advice and assistance: Mike Ashley, Ian Covell, Richard Dalby, Eric Held, Margaret Henry, Steven Moore, Frank H. Parnell, Martin V. Riccardo, Giovanni Scognamillo, and Marlene Wood.

Brian J. Frost

Part One
Guises of the Vampire:
An Inventory

The Origins of the Vampire Myth

By many names, and in a host of disparate guises, the vampire has been known to men of all nations throughout history. Indeed, so immeasurably ancient is this polymorphic phenomenon that its origins can be traced back through all the ages of which there are records preserved, until they become lost in the twilight of tradition and fable. Consequently, any attempt to find the forgotten source of the legends surrounding the vampire inevitably leads the researcher down the hazardous path of conjecture.

If, for instance, we accept the proposition that the belief in vampires and bloodsucking demons is as old as man himself, it might be reasonable to suppose that the concept of the vampire was conceived in the minds of certain individuals in prehistoric times, and has subsequently become part of the collective subconscious of the human race. On the other hand, there is a distinct possibility that vampires, along with other equally ancient symbols of terror, are of much older standing, and are, as Algernon Blackwood once speculated, "survivals of a hugely remote period when consciousness was manifested in shapes and forms long since withdrawn before the tide of advancing humanity."

Should the latter proposition be correct, then the original incarnation of the vampire might well have been as an obscene, parasitic entity of supermundane size and grotesque outline, which ravened and fought with the other grisly prototypes of terrene life in the primordial ooze—something, I like to imagine, not unlike the monster-god in A. Merritt's classic fantasy novel *Dwellers in the Mirage*. A thing of awful force and of a potential destructiveness almost beyond finite comprehension, it is described thus:

Khalk'ru was the Beginning—without Beginning, as he would be the End—without End. He was the lightless Timeless Void; the Destroyer; the Eater-up of Life: The Annihilator. The Dissolver! He was not Death—Death was only part of him. He was alive, very much so, but his quality of living was the antithesis of life as we know it.

Unsurpassed as the most awesome fictional incarnation of the vampire, Khalk'ru is the symbolic embodiment of the primal hidden horror that festers at the root of being—what the Ancients called the Feeder, the All.

Whether the inspiration for such a terrifying monster came purely from Merritt's fertile imagination, or was inspired by a racial memory that had somehow impinged on his consciousness, we will never know; but psychologists assure us that somewhere in the *terra incognita* of the brain is a hidden storehouse of ancestral memories reaching back to those of the hairy, ape-like ancestors who preceded man, and even beyond them to those of the amphibious creatures who crawled out of the steaming swamps to begin their slow evolution into *Homo sapiens*— and perhaps still farther back to *their* ancestors. In fact, it may well be that the entire experience of biological life from its earliest manifestations is conserved and comprised in all its detail in the racial memory of every individual, waiting to be tapped. If so, then surely it is in this hidden compartment of our minds—the collective unconscious, as Jung has called it—that we must search for the forerunner of the vampire...if we dare!

Occasionally, however, an awareness of the forgotten memories submerged in the archaic levels of the mind can come unbidden through the gate of slumber. For it is when we are dreaming that the mind is most receptive to primitive emotions and fears; and in our nightmares we sometimes catch brief, distorted glimpses of life as it was untold millions of years ago, when the likes of Khalk'ru ruled the world. Fortunately, by the time the first primitive men appeared on earth any factual counterparts of this nightmarish monster which may have existed were long extinct. But this did not mean that life for our early ancestors was made any easier by their prior departure. On the contrary, primitive man found himself thrust into an unfriendly world acrawl with feral life. During the daytime there were ferocious predators and the untamed forces of primal nature to contend with, and at night the even more daunting forces of darkness and the Unseen. Thus, with good cause, primitive man was very much in awe of his surroundings, and anything he could not explain was classed as supernatural.

In particular did our ancient forebear fear the approach of nightfall, for then the terrors which beset him would be multiplied a thousand-fold as the darkness transformed the landscape into shadowy shapes of dim, uncertain outline, suggesting to his rampant imagination a million intimations of amorphous, half-revealed phantoms. Even in the comparative safety of his rude dwelling there was no escape from the vast primeval dread which embraced him in its icy grip. For there, also, the hidden horrors of the "living" darkness made their presence felt, clamoring at the cave entrance for admittance, held back only by the purifying flames of the fire that barred their way. Nor would sleep offer a sure means of escape either, since it invariably brought with it terror-filled dreams in which a horde of unbodied phantoms sought to impress themselves on the dreamer's consciousness, leaving his imagination to clothe them in flesh—a flesh so much more hideous than anything even primal nature could fashion.

Thus, ironically, it was the same devine gift of imagination which had set man above the other primates that betrayed him into so many false beliefs. Yet one must concede its inevitability, for when a primitive, unbridled imagination attempts to analyse things beyond its comprehension it invariably constructs all kinds of false interpretations. Thus one is drawn to the conclusion that the concept of the demonic vampire—the nocturnal, bloodsucking fiend of non-human origin—stems from our forebears' ignorance of how to distinguish dreams and other strange fancies from reality. Bearing this in mind, it is not surprising that primitive societies the world over should have created whole pantheons of gods and demons, all supposedly out to gorge themselves on human flesh and blood.

Vampires of the Ancient World

By the beginning of the historical era the vampire was a well-established denizen of the demon world, appearing in a variety of guises. Records left by the ancient Assyrians and Babylonians confirm that vampirish demons were a great menace to the people of those times. The most feared of all were the Seven Spirits, a consortium of tyrannical, blood-quaffing demon-gods who rampaged throughout the countryside causing havoc. A modern translation of cuneiform inscriptions describes them in the following colorful manner:

> They range against mankind:
> They spill blood like rain,
> Devouring their flesh (and) sucking their veins.

One of the earliest female vampires on record is the Babylonian snake-goddess Lilitu, who was later borrowed by the Hebrews for their own traditional lore and renamed Lilith. According to the Talmud it was no less a personage than Adam, our traditional progenitor, who mated with her and begot flesh-eating devils. Rabbinical doctrine further states that the she-monster Lilith was conceived out of Adam's voluptuous imaginings, coming to him in his dreams as a succubus. In Hebrew mythology the succubi and their male counterparts, the incubi, were originally a band of fallen angels who had degenerated into lecherous night demons. The incubi appeared to the fair sex as demon lovers and the succubi similarly haunted the dreams of young men, magically undermining their vitality and draining their potency.

In the Classical World the demonic vampire was nearly always of the feminine gender. For instance, the male population of ancient Greece were plagued by lascivious, fur-breasted vampiresses known as Empusae; and in Pagan Rome the serpent-bodied Lamia, a vicious demoness capable of transforming herself into a seductive courtesan, lured youths into her cruel embrace for the dual purpose of sating her carnal lust and draining her victims' life-blood.

Besides the demon variety, vampires of human origin also plagued the peoples of the Ancient World. The chief aggressor in this respect was the Ekimmu, an evil spirit of a dead person which sought to regain its former earthly existence at the expense of the living. This it did by sucking out its victims' vitality in a ghastly reversal of the kiss of life. The ancient Egyptians, too, feared the return of the vengeful dead. This was all bound up with their belief that the astral double imprisoned in the mummified corpse must have regular nourishment; and if this was not provided it could result in a simulacrum of the deceased issuing from the tomb on an errand for blood, which it usually stole from those who had neglected their funereal duties.

Blood, Diablerie, and Undeath

Moving a step further on in history one finds many references in Anglo-Saxon and Norse chronicles to the return of the bloodthirsting dead. Mention, too, is made of the ritual imbibing of blood, which was, according to pagan blood-lore, supposed to possess magical properties— hence the Vikings' gruesome tradition of drinking the blood of their dead foes in order to acquire greater military prowess.

In the Middle Ages and throughout the Renaissance the demonic vampire spread its blight across the face of Europe, even invading the sanctity of the Church. Indeed, such was the extent of the infestation within the hallowed walls of holy edifices that one can only guess at the number of virgin nuns who were seduced by lustful incubi, or how many celibate monks succumbed to the illicit caresses of deliciously-curved succubi. But many there must have been if we are to believe the dubious findings of the notorious medieval witchcraft and heresy trials.

According to occultists, succuba-demons sometimes have an objective existence and can take on a tangible form, the substance of which they are formed being a projection of the substance of the person to whom they appear. Though initially thin and shadowy, these insatiable night vampires grow denser by feeding off the life-principle of their creators, whom they increasingly dominate, sometimes destroying them with the ardor of their passion. However, in spite of the fact that they were cited as the devil's agents in medieval courts, it is apparent to us today, in the light of modern psychology, that these nightmare demons were in reality manifestations of the unconscious, i.e. projections of inner desires in the victims themselves which came to life only when suppressed or violent emotions—usually of a sexual nature—called them into being. This being the case, it follows that the alleged power of succuba-demons depended upon mass psychology, and they only became powerful through the use of mental energy emanating from credulous people *en masse* in the form of hideous creative imagination.

By the 17th century, belief in demonic vampires had waned considerably; but this did not mean that the inhabitants of Europe's remoter regions slept any easier in their beds, as a new menace to body and soul had emerged in the form of the Undead. If we are to believe the legends, the Undead are among the most formidable monsters in the entire supernatural domain, possessing several attributes that make them virtually indestructible during the hours of darkness. To enumerate them: they have superhuman strength; they are masters of disguise and can assume a variety of forms, either to deceive their prey or escape detection; and they are adept in the art of hypnotism, which they use to subjugate their victims. Only during the daytime are they vulnerable, and then only staking, decapitation, or burning can break the vampire's hold on his house of flesh.

The essential characteristic of an "undead" vampire, apart from the obvious one of originating from a deceased person, is his disgusting habit of sucking the blood of the living and relying exclusively on this diet for sustenance. Like a drug addict he needs his nightly "fix" of blood for survival; it is his food and drink, his staff of life.

Ruthless, self-centered, and without a trace of kindness or pity, a person who has become one of the Undead by choice leads a degenerate, inhuman existence: one without love or honor; one devoid of even the slightest friendship—even among his own kind. Moreover, because vampirism is contagious, the victims of the vampire's bite are also drawn into the same undead state, and thenceforward are forced to do the bidding of "The Master", who in return offers them only a ghastly pseudo-life in exchange for their souls. Thus the serene look observed on the faces of the vampire's victims after staking is seen as evidence that they welcome the release from their enforced bondage. So, in this respect, vampirism can be likened to a disease which is transmitted from one person to another in virus form, leading to death and undeath, interment and resurrection, from the initial infection to eternity.

Arising from the points made so far, two questions beg an answer: (1) Why does the "true" vampire willingly choose this horrible life-in-death?; and (2) Why is blood the sole nourishment of all those who join the ranks of the Undead? The answer to the first question is, I believe, that "true" vampires are, above all, people in revolt against the inevitable principle of corporeal death. Having led extremely evil lives they know only too well the dreadful fate awaiting them in the after-life, and are prepared to go to any lengths to sustain a semblance of life in their bodies in order to remain earthbound. Therefore it follows that the only alternative to death is to become one of the Undead. With regard to the question of the vampire's peculiar dining habits, one is forced, through lack of an alternative, to fall back on the popular belief in the magical powers attributed to blood as the only possible reason for the vampire's singular craving for this vital fluid. For as any occult manual will tell you, blood is the liquid source of life, as efficacious in aiding revivification and rejuvenation as it is in creating new tissue. To put it in a nutshell: food can maintain life, but only blood can renew it.

Occultists, along with the various spiritualist societies, have always insisted that there is a terribly serious substratum of truth behind the eerie legend of the vampire, and to support their claims have advanced several intriguing theories to account for the phenomenon. Theosophists—adherents of the Wisdom-Religion founded by H. P. Blavatsky—maintain that the hideous anachronisms we call vampires are, in fact, appalling relics of a time long ago when this planet was populated by the bestial fourth root-race. Their belief is that although modern man, who belongs to the fifth root-race, has evolved beyond the cannibalistic ways of his early ancestors, legacies of his brutish past still crop up today in parts of Eastern Europe, where there is still a considerable strain of the ancient fourth-race blood.

After years of increasing virulence, the human vampire reached a pinnacle of gory activity in the late seventeenth and early eighteenth centuries; and in the rural areas of south-east Europe their nocturnal perambulations spread fear and panic among the predominantly-peasant population. Following this outbreak of vampire mania, accounts of "authentic", fully-attested cases of vampirism were collected in copious volumes; but in our more skeptical age it has become fashionable to dismiss these as the result of mass hysteria, or attribute their source to the over-ripe imaginations of credulous peasants. The medical profession, for example, has suggested that the vampire phenomenon was a false diagnosis of what were really cases of premature burial. However, while this may apply in most cases, there is still a small percentage of occurrences which cannot be explained away by rational theories; and it is these that have kept the "undead" vampire a topic of speculation up to this day.

Spirit-Vampires

Though undoubtedly the most popular, the description of the human vampire as a dead body actuated by fearsome life which physically attacks its victims is not the only one to be considered here. There is also a widely-held theory that it is the vampire's spectral double or semi-materialized simulacrum which issues from the grave at night on its grisly errand, whilst the corpse lies inert in its coffin in a cataleptic trance, preserved indefinitely from decomposition by the horrible expedient of the transfusion of fresh blood drawn from the veins of the living. This particular theory would seem to be connected with the widespread belief among primitive people that, under certain propitious circumstances, souls of the dead can return to the world of the living, either for love or revenge. Revenants, as the shades of the returning dead are called, are characterized by their fugitiveness and fantastic changeability. In appearance they are said to resemble thin, shadowy human images, and though impalpable still manifest physical power as well as possessing the personality and volition they had in their former corporeal state. Thus, when enforced by concentrated will—consciousness having been transferred from the defunct physical shell—they can leave the corpse far behind, flashing swiftly from place to place in their quest for sustenance.

Occultists have expressed a similar belief to that just described, but refer to the spectral image of a dead person as the etheric double. Man, they maintain, has *two* bodies—the dense material one (i.e. the shell of flesh) and a subtle astral body which permeates the corporeal body and acts as the vehicle of the life forces. Though invisible in the daytime to all but the ultra-psychic, the earthbound astral form of a dead person is sometimes visible in the dark. In appearance it is vaguely luminous, like a silver mist composed of tiny particles which twist and crawl upon themselves.

Actually, the idea that man has two bodies is not so outrageous as it may seem. After all, it certainly ties in with the dualistic nature of man. To state the obvious: we have two eyes, two ears, a duplicity of limbs, and internal organs paired or divided in two. In a way we even have two minds—the conscious and the subconscious . So the idea of two bodies does not seem contrary to the order of things. In fact, if we carry this line of reasoning still further we can find a duality about the main forces in man's life, inasmuch as mankind is constantly torn between two opposites: Love and Hate, Good and Evil, God and the Devil, Life and Death—and in the potential vampire's case it boils down to a straight choice between death and undeath.

What happens to us after death has always been a topic for speculation. Occultists, who have always had a lot to say on the subject, claim that when a person dies the astral body containing the soul draws out of the physical form and drifts about the neighborhood of the corpse for approximately three days. Then, at the conclusion of this period, the soul draws out of the astral body, which, in turn, dies, and the liberated soul enters upon the second phase of posthumous existence. However, the Second Death, as this is called, is feared by all evildoers; for then must come the final reckoning when their wicked earth-lives will be judged. And so great is the arch-sinner's fear of this inevitability, so chained is he to earth by gross desires of the flesh, that he is ready to go to any lengths to avoid the punishment due to him—even if this means becoming a spirit-vampire.

Putting this desperate plan into action entails taking over the body of a living organism, either animal or human, and establishing a rapport with the subconscious mind of the chosen victim, who is then provoked into committing acts of vampirism. This way the spirit-vampire is able to secure a regular source of nourishment, the victim becoming, in effect, a human feeding-bottle for the vampire that holds him in its power. Moreover, because vampirism is contagious, the spirit-vampire can systematically draw its nutriment over a long period without killing off its victim; for he, in turn, is vampirizing someone else to resupply the blood being extracted from his body. In short: it's a vicious circle.

In some cases, however, the spirit-vampire prefers to materialize rather than submerge itself in the form of its host. The following graphic scene from Dion Fortune's novel *The Demon Lover*, in which a young woman is the victim of vampirism, describes how this is achieved:

For a while she lay in a dreamy, somnolent state that was not unpleasant, then a new sensation made itself felt, as if something were being drawn out of her left side, at first a trickling, then a strange draining sensation, and she saw a white, mistlike pool spread out, which rose up, took form in front of her in the semblance of a tenuous, sheeted ghost, and then, in a dark hollow of the draperies, a face began to form, and it was the face of Lucas!

Veronica, drained of vitality, lay back in her chair, and saw the dead man take life before her. The bright, dark eyes gazed into her clouded ones; the lips, red with life-blood, drew close to her pallid ones; and the arms, strong as in life, closed round her form that seemed all shrunken inside her clothes.

What is actually happening here is that part of the girl's substance has been drained from her to build up the vampire's form. In a later materialization the vampire appears in an even more horrible guise: this time the ghostly form shines phosphorescently and the draperies are spread out into great bat-like wings tipped with claws.

Vampires of the Astral Plane

To my mind, the most fascinating theories about spirit-vampires are those expounded by the Theosophists. Among other strange beliefs, they hold that the planet Earth is surrounded and enclosed by an invisible region made up of the dregs of spirit-substance, called the Astral Light. This, they say, is the storehouse of cosmic life-energy and the receptacle of whatever passes out of the physical sphere, including all the vile and horrible emanations from earth and earth-beings.

As far as after-life existence is concerned, Theosophists believe that when a person dies he lays aside his physical body and enters the astral plane to begin the first stage of his postmortem existence. All the sphere's evil residents are confined to the seventh and lowest subdivision of the astral plane, which might, for want of a better analogy, be equated with the Purgatory of Christianity or the Hades of Greek mythology. Sometimes called the Desire-World, the ancient Egyptians knew the astral plane as Amenti, the Land of Silent Shadows. An ancient Papyrus describes it thus: "It hath no water, it hath no air; it is deep, unfathomable; it is black as the blackest night, and men wander helplessly therein." C. W. Leadbeater, a leading Theosophist of this century, has added the following details: "There appears to be a sense of density and gross materiality about it which is indescribably loathsome to the liberated astral body, causing it the sense of pushing its way through some black viscous fluid, while the inhabitants and influences encountered there are also usually exceedingly undesirable."

Apparently, in this strange, illusory world the familiar and the outré merge and mingle. The scenery, for example, is like that of earth as we know it but grotesquely distorted, inasmuch as there are no horizons and no perspective, only varying densities and ever-shifting contours. Colors, too, are absent, as the bleak terrain is continually bathed in a glaucous, semi-aqueous light, which gives everything a monotonous, verminous-gray coloring. Worst of all, wherever one wanders in this dreary limbo there is a sense of uncanny menace. This applies particularly to the lower regions, which are no less than the source and repository of all miscreation and abomination. For here dwell the multitudinous and multiform horrors of our nightmares: vampires, werewolves, and a whole host of unearthly, nameless entities, all of them inimical to mankind.

Fortunately, the only disembodied human egos to have a conscious existence on the lower levels of the astral plane are those of ex-persons whose earth-lives have been exceptionally vile and evil. In such people the desires of the flesh remain strong even after death, and unless they can work off these base lusts during their enforced sojourn on the astral plane they are liable to develop into terribly evil entities inflamed with all kinds of horrible appetites. There are, however, certain limitations placed on the plane's more unsavory denizens, as their evil passions—

which may have been easily satisfied on earth—can now only be gratified vicariously on the rare occasions when they are able to batten onto a like-minded person on the physical plane. After possessing him, they take a devilish delight in using all the arts of delusion which the astral plane puts in their power to lead their victim into the same excesses which have proved so fatal to themselves.

The ultimate horror of life-after-death is reserved for those who have lived a life of utter degradation. It is said that a person with no redeeming feature whatsoever attains a pre-eminence in evil which could, in an exceptional case, entail the complete loss of personality, turning that person into a "living corpse." After death, this lost soul would be unable to stay even in the lowest division of the astral plane, but would be irresistibly drawn into the mysterious Eighth Sphere, the terrible limbo of the lost known, alternatively, as the Planet of Death. There, after experiences too horrible to contemplate, the astral shell of the evildoer would slowly disintegrate until its final and irreversible extinction.

Not all the wandering, bodiless entities of the Beyond which prey vampirishly upon the living are of human origin. If we are to believe Theosophists and other students of Eastern occultism, there is an enormous inchoate mass of invisible, soulless intelligences which hover, black-hearted and hungry, within contact of our plane of existence, ever eager to cross the boundary of the unmanifest and gain a footing on the plane of life. Of greater magnitude than the rest and having an inveterate hatred of the human race are a class of vicious, aggressive spirits with vampirish propensities called vice-elementals. Often equated with the demons of Antiquity, they are really primal earth forces that have not evolved along the evolutionary scale. To put it another way, they are only fractions of true entities—mere illusions without any core of substance in themselves. But they are cunning and clever despite their subhuman mentality; and in pursuit of their single, all-absorbing desire— to steal or make for themselves a living body—they show infinite patience and resource.

When an elemental breaks through the fragile veil that separates the spirit world from the world of the living it becomes manifest by drawing the necessary life-force for materialization from a suitable human source, preferably from someone in a state of low resistance. This could be somebody who is sick or wounded, or even insane; but the ideal victim is a person of a negative character who is easily manipulated. After possessing the mind of its chosen victim, the elemental draws out the subtle ether from his body to build itself a visible form; and when fully materialized is usually semi-human or half animal in appearance, or has an extremely grotesque form—like, for instance, a giant slug. The wretched victim, on the other hand, meets a horrible death; for the elemental, finding its devitalized victim useless, vents all its hate upon him by rending the last drop of life from his body with vicious force, and then casts aside the twisted shell of what was once a human being and sets off to begin similar operations upon a fresh victim. Now able to move with extraordinary rapidity, the fully materialized elemental may eventually become capable of enormous and destructive power, which can only be measured by the amount of life-force it is able to draw from its human sources of supply. In other words: the more people it vampirizes, the more powerful it becomes.

Certain elementals are attracted by blood, and are said to hover about the scene of gory accidents or among the carnage of a battlefield. In *Isis Unveiled*, H. P. Blavatsky wrote that "blood begets phantoms and its emanations furnish certain spirits with the material required to fashion their temporary appearance." Commenting on the same issue, the famous ghost-hunter, Elliott O'Donnell, maintained that for a more prolonged existence on the physical plane an elemental would have to appropriate an untenanted body. His definition of a vampire is: "an elemental that under certain conditions inhabits a dead body, whether human or otherwise, and thus incarcerated comes out of the grave at night to suck the blood of a living person." Yet another viewpoint has been expressed by Rollo Ahmed, author of *The Black Art*. According to him, elementals are "quasi-intelligent thought creations which feed upon the evil thoughts, passions and lusts which emanate from a living person." Theosophists go even further and suggest that elemental essence—an invisible substance which, so they say, surrounds us on every side—is susceptible to the influence of human thought, especially concentrated thought of a purposeful kind. It follows, therefore, that a strong-willed person could seize upon this plastic essence and mold it into an artificial elemental—a sort of astral attendant. But the danger is that evil thoughts, once given form, feast upon their creators and become vile guests in the house of the mind. And the chances are that this "thought vampire", if constantly fed by fresh thought, would haunt its creator for years, gaining an increasing degree of influence over him, so that eventually it could induce him to commit acts of vampirism, and might ultimately possess him entirely. On the other hand, a trained manipulator versed in the practices of lower magic could send this "thought vampire" to hover over someone he had a grudge against. But for anyone so disposed, the great nineteenth-century magician, Eliphas Levi, has the following warning: "When one creates phantoms for oneself, one puts vampires into the world, and one must nourish these children of voluntary nightmare with one's blood, one's life, one's intelligence, and one's reason, without ever satisfying them."

Black magicians have, reputedly, a considerable power over spirits, and are said to be capable of calling into existence artificial elementals of extreme virulence and power. According to Paracelsus, an Adept can call forth any spirit he desires to see from the fumes of blood. Nevertheless, there is always the risk that these evil spirits might escape the control of their masters and enjoy an independent existence, sustaining their vitality by vampirizing human beings. They may even be sufficiently powerful to seize upon and inhabit some passing astral shell (i.e. astral corpses in the later stages of disintegration, from which all that is spiritual has departed). The vitalized shell, as it is then called, serves as a temporary home for the elemental, enabling it to commit acts of vampirism more easily, and so prolong its existence on the physical plane.

Perhaps the last word on the subject of elementals and the like should be left to Eliphas Levi, who, though he was steeped in occult lore, was still honest enough to make the following admission: "Human thought creates what it imagines; the phantoms of superstition project their real deformity in the Astral Light, and live by the very terrors they produce. They owe their being to the delusions of imagination and the aberration of the senses, and are never produced in the presence of anyone who knows and can expose the mystery of their monstrous birth."

Real-Life Vampires

A class of human vampires quite distinct from any of those described so far are real-life vampires, who are also sometimes called "living" vampires. Lacking any supernatural powers whatsoever, such people are strictly speaking sadistic criminals whose vampirish atrocities are urged on by a physical craving for blood which is so urgent and devouring that it demands to be appeased no matter what degradations it leads to. Indeed, so obsessed are these blood-crazed psychopaths with the idea that blood is the primal life force, and with its ingestion life can be extended beyond its normal bounds, that in their mad quest for the forbidden "red milk" they torture, mutilate, and eventually murder their wretched victims. But by the time they discover that blood is not the magic elixir they supposed it to be, and is unable to grant them immortality, they have become "hooked" on its rich taste and cannot live without it.

Real-life vampires whose gory crimes have gained them a lasting notoriety include Gilles de Rais, Peter Kürten, and John George Haigh. Vivid accounts of their sanguinary careers, and those of other mass-murderers who were similarly motivated, can be found in Cliff Howe's *Scoundrels, Fiends & Human Monsters* (1958), R. M. Ebeling's *The Vampire in Human Form* (1961), Raymond Rudorff's *Monsters* (1968), and Don Glut's *True Vampires of History* (1971). Two books which focus on one particular historical figure are *The Bloody Countess* (1974) by Valentine Penrose and *Dracula Was a Woman* (1983) by Raymond T. McNally. Both catalog the crimes of Elizabeth Bathory, the 16th-century Hungarian countess whose depraved sensuality manifested itself in her habit of bathing in the blood of slaughtered virgins, which she mistakenly believed would stave off old age and keep her skin smooth and white. Unbelievably, her inordinate vanity claimed the lives of over six hundred young girls.

Looking into the motivation behind such atrocities, Gabriel Ronay (author of *The Dracula Myth*) observes that the sight of the flow of blood and human suffering can, to some psychologically damaged persons, cause ecstatic pleasure; and he draws the conclusion that the hidden motive behind most sexual crimes is the desire to shed blood. Personally, I believe there is an even more sinister explanation for the excesses of perverts like Gilles de Rais and Elizabeth Bathory. Without question they were both guilty of gross criminal acts, but in a way they were also victims. For, far from being totally wicked, I think it is more likely that they were driven on by urges beyond their control, and that a probable explanation for their crimes is that an atavistic strain hidden deep within them was awoken into vile response at some traumatic stage in their lives, so that thenceforward they were forced, out of sheer impulse, to kill or shed blood. (N.B. Atavism is an outcropping of tendencies and characteristics that have skipped two generations or more, but in a "living" vampire's case may have lain dormant, skipping dozens of generations and reappearing only after many centuries of extinction.)

Psychic Vampires

The subtlest form of vampirism practiced by human beings on their fellows is psychic vampirism, which is a mysterious process whereby certain persons are able to steal other people's vitality without even touching them. By no means a clever literary invention, as one might suppose, psychic vampires really exist. Moreover, they are the least detectable vampires of all, as the vitality-stealing process is invariably an unconscious and involuntary act. Therefore, not only is the "vampire" often unaware of his/her fatal powers, but the victim also has little inkling of the real cause of his/her gradual decline in health.

Madame Blavatsky, the famous Victorian mystic, once described this particular brand of vampirism as "a kind of occult osmosis," adding in typically pretentious nomenclature that "the agent of transmission is a magnetic and attractive faculty, terrestrial and psychological in its results, yet generated and produced on the 'four-dimensional plane'— the realm of atoms." But if you find this difficult to understand, then Dion Fortune's version of the process should clarify the situation. In one of her books, *Psychic Self Defense*, she explains that what is really happening is that the negative partner of such a liaison is "shorting" on the positive partner, resulting in a leakage of vitality, which the "absorber" is, consciously or unconsciously, lapping up.

In practice, psychic parasitism—to give the condition its correct name—usually takes the form of a morbid attachment between two people of widely different temperaments, with the stronger of the two devitalizing the weaker one. The classic case is the near-lesbianic bond between a young girl and an older woman. The latter—always the dominant partner—absorbs the vitality of her young, vigorous companion, leaving her, in the course of time, an empty sucked-out husk, while she, the absorber, has gained for herself a kind of pseudo-youth.

Psychic sponges who misuse their powers for evil ends have, like all vampires, a possessive nature where their victims are concerned. Their strategy is to concentrate on one person at a time, spending a long time patiently studying them and monopolizing their company. Only when they have gained complete control over the victim's will do they press home the attack.

During these periods of psychic aggression the victim, who is always someone of a nervous disposition in the first place, becomes even more highly strung, to the point where he or she becomes the very personification of neurosis. The typical symptoms observed in someone being vampirized in this way are extreme sensitivity, a pallid complexion, a wasted form, and general debility. They are also highly suggestible and easily influenced. Needless to say, unless the victims can be separated from the magnetic aura of the psychic vampire their fate is a lingering death.

Forms of psychic vampirism of an even more bizarre nature have also been detected. There is, for instance, a school of thought which holds that the influence of evil deeds and evil thoughts may persist and even accumulate in certain places long after the originators have passed away. This has led some psychic investigators to speculate that, in suitable conditions, the human mind can amalgamate with inorganic substances. Indeed, some report that they have actually come across instances where this has occurred—in the form of ancient, half-animate houses that have a vampiric influence on their occupants. The experts in such matters describe this rare occurrence as the materialization of the Animate Force through the Inanimate Inert, which in layman's terms means that a continuity of malignant thought has, over a long period of time, produced a positive action upon the immediate surrounding material, so that in some inexplicable way the very masonry making up the structure of the building has become imbued with an evil, life-sapping force, which could eventually grow into a manifestation of awesome power.

Similarly, old graveyards and prehistoric burial-places teem with the terrible, unbodied intelligence of past generations. Psychic investigators claim that thoughts of a malign nature which have been long dwelt on and have outlived the dead human systems that gave them birth can gain a mysterious vitality through an interaction with psychic germs, which enables them to attract to themselves suitable elements from the environment in order to materialize and so carry out their evil desires.

According to Elliott O'Donnell, who was the author of dozens of books on the supernatural, ancient hillside barrows are especially propitious for the creation of vampires of both demonic and human origin. His pet theory about tomb-spawned vampires was that they choose babies or young children for victims, sucking their brain cells dry of intellect with their superphysical mouths and reducing them to grinning, anemic idiots, who, in turn, become vampires by drawing mental sustenance from the healthy brains around them. True or not, it's a frightening thought.

Animal Vampires
Vampirism is not the sole preserve of human or demonic vampires,

but in one kind or another may be said to leave its trace throughout almost all of nature. There are, for instance, animal vampires of various sorts, of which the South American vampire bat is probably the best-known. Deriving its name from feeding habits which closely resemble those of the vampire of European folklore, the vampire bat attacks cattle and other livestock, and has even been known to suck the blood of sleeping human beings, often infecting them with rabies.

Two other animals closely associated with vampirism are the wolf and the cat. Traditionally, vampires have the power to make wolves do their bidding, and when it suits their purpose can assume lupine form themselves. Feline vampires, on the other hand, usually crop up in connection with witchcraft; and in medieval times it was thought that witches transformed themselves into cats in order to suck the blood of children. Also, I need hardly remind you that black cats were the favorite pets of witches. In fact, many of these hapless creatures were, believe it or not, tried and burnt at the stake for "practicing black magic," all because they were thought to be the witch's personal demon in disguise. The prime duty of a familiar, as a demonic servant of this class was called, was to aid the witch in her magic, for which it was rewarded by being allowed to suck blood from a small protuberance or supernumerary nipple on the witch's body, commonly known as "the witch's mark."

Other species of the earth's fauna have, on occasion, exhibited vampirish tendencies—snakes, frogs, owls, butterflies, moths, and a button-sized, parasitic crustacean called the Argulus, to name but a few. But the most curious to my mind is a microscopic protoplasm known as the Vampyrella Spirogyra: a simple red cell, formless and almost structureless, which rejects all food in its environment except an aquatic plant called Spirogyra, which it hunts for, breaks into one of its cells, and sucks the contents dry.

Contemporary Vampires

The current vampire craze has been of considerable duration, and contrary to expectations has shown no sign of tailing off. It began as far back as the late sixties, when interest in the vampire phenomenon was dramatically revived by a much-publicized search for the truth behind the Dracula legend, the findings from which were subsequently presented to the public in several books and dozens of magazine articles. Since then various research groups have been formed, bringing together, in an informal network, people from different countries dedicated to the collection and dissemination of information pertaining to all aspects of vampirism.

According to Stephen Kaplan, the founder and director of The Vampire Research Center in New York, contemporary vampires fall into three main categories: genuine vampires who have a chemical or physical need for fresh blood, vampire-like people with a psychopathological fixation about blood, and psychic vampires. Kaplan, who is probably the most publicized vampirologist in America today, keeps tabs on the growth of the vampire population by conducting a census at regular intervals, and estimates that at the time of the one taken in 1986 there were up to 200 genuine vampires at large in the United States and Canada, and about 500 worldwide. His estimate of the number of vampiroids— people who think they are vampires, or have similar characteristics— is less precise, but he reckons there are between 10,000 and 20,000 resident in North America, and probably as many as 100,000 worldwide.

Replies to questionnaires circulated among the vampire community in the United States have revealed that there is little to distinguish a vampire from a normal person as far as looks are concerned. However, significant genetic and metabolic differences have been uncovered, including abnormalities in body temperature and chemical balance, and an apparent slowing down of the biological clock.

If one pools the findings of Kaplan with those of other contemporary American vampirologists, the following description of the average male "genetic" vampire emerges: He has blond hair and blue eyes, is 5 ft. 10 ins. tall, and weighs around 150 pounds. Distinguishing features include very pale skin, fang-like teeth, and an absence of facial hair. He also has a highly developed sense of smell, but less sense of taste than a normal person; and, besides being incredibly strong, is double-jointed and can run very fast. His genito-urinary system is similar to that of a human being, but the semen is pink and the urine has a reddish hue. Life expectancy is between 400 and 500 years.

Edwin Austin, who runs the Mutilation Data Center in Washington, has also done some original research on vampirism and related matters. Currently, he is trying to discover the relationship between livestock mutilation and vampirism, and has made public some of his findings in a paper titled *A Cattle Mutilation Theory*, which claims that livestock mutilation has reached epidemic proportions in parts of the United States.

A mystery yet to be solved is that examination of the blood-drained carcasses has revealed high levels of a little-known tranquillizer, and any animal corpses so treated are always left untouched by scavengers.

Lonely, estranged, and often persecuted, vampires have always tended to keep a low profile, seeking anonymity in environments that minimize the risk of detection and maximize the opportunity to obtain a regular supply of blood. Today the favorite haunts of vampires are the squalid alleys and back-streets of run-down, inner-city neighborhoods, where, under the cover of darkness, they prey on those whom society least cares about—runaways, derelicts, the old and the sick. There is evidence, however, that recent trends in social and sexual behavior have enabled the more enterprising members of the vampire community to widen their circle of victims. In California, for instance, young, attractive-looking vampires are reported to be cruising singles bars looking for innocent victims for depraved blood rituals, whilst others are rumored to have infiltrated Satanic and pseudo-religious cults.

Recently, a connection between necrophilia and vampirism was acknowledged with the disclosure by Leilah Wendell, founder of the American Association of Necrophiliac Research and Enlightenment, that members of her organization practice what they call vampiristic romance. This involves drinking blood from a fresh corpse as the climax to the act of necrophiliac love. It may sound revolting, but Ms. Wendell euphemistically describes it as "a reverent psychic ceremony," and insists that necrophilia is basically a spiritual experience transcending any thoughts of sexual gratification.

Apologists for vampires are quick to point out that not all blood-drinkers behave in the same way as the few "bad apples" who hit the headlines. Most vampires, they insist, are not the menace to society they are made out to be, but are themselves the victims of ignorance and prejudice. In the eyes of this growing band of sympathisers, genetic vampires—or Sangroids as they prefer to be called—are harmless predators who use seduction and hypnotism to obtain what they need, taking only token amounts of blood from willing donors.

Strangely enough, despite all the interest shown in vampires throughout history, no completely satisfactory explanation of the phenomenon has yet been established. Needless to say, this has not stopped people from formulating their own pet theories. Recently, Dr. David Dolphin, a chemistry professor at the University of British Colombia, advanced the theory that people who exhibit vampirish traits are suffering from a rare genetic blood disorder called porphyria, symptoms of which are extreme sensitivity to sunlight, excessive hairiness, and a tautness around the lips and gums, which makes the teeth more prominent. On the other hand, John L. Vellutini, editor of *The Journal of Vampirology*, is equally convinced that vampirism is due to the activity of a certain pathogenic anerobic bacteria, the bacillus responsible being a member of the clostridium family. There has also been some speculation in recent years about the possible existence of a specific gene-cracking virus which induces a craving for blood in certain individuals, but is otherwise beneficial to their systems, bringing about longevity and resistance to disease. Others have argued that the elucidation of the mystery should be sought primarily in the hidden world of the sleeping psyche—the place wherein imagination finds its models.

Those who favor this last hypothesis have, one suspects, been greatly influenced by the psychoanalytical observations of Carl Jung, in particular his theory that everyone shares in a vast, vague racial inheritance of cosmic memories which have been engraved upon the mind from one generation to the next. Defined by Jung as Archetypes, these indelible images are thought to be a legacy or residue of the function of the animal ancestral chain of humanity, representing the accumulated experience of organic existence on earth. Although normally buried deep in the dark labyrinths of the unconscious, they can sometimes manifest themselves in conscious life as personalized dream images. In other words, they are the monsters and other strange, disturbing figures—like the vampire—that constantly appear in our nightmares.

Of course, psychology must always be an area of speculation rather than hard facts, but at least Jung's ingenious theory would explain why the vampire superstition repeats itself the world over, and also why it has such a strong hold on the imaginations of every new generation. But, above all, it would make apparent to everyone that the underlying fear and detestation we have for the vampire is caused by our subconscious awareness of it as an ancient, universal memory. Even so, confirmation of this would still not bring us peace of mind, for then we would have to live with the rather daunting thought that the vampire is an undying fear-image which will haunt our dreams forever.

The most sensational theories about vampires are those that link them with the UFO phenomenon. UFO trackers report that the blood-drained corpses of animals are often found on terrain over which UFOs have been sighted, leading to speculation that mysterious visitors from outer space are to blame. There was even a report in the *National Enquirer* not so long ago which claimed that vampires from space had caused a "reign of terror" in Brazil, paralyzing their victims with blinding light, then sucking out their blood.

Whilst media reports of this kind are readily dismissed as colorful fabrications by all but the most credulous, there are, it would seem, a growing number of people who are willing to accept recent claims that several allegedly genuine vampires have made contact with various individuals and groups sympathetic to their condition. However, as a detached observer, fully aware that charlatanism has been a characteristic of even the most celebrated figures connected with the study of paranormal phenomena, I tend to be highly skeptical of these unsubstantiated reports. Nevertheless, one can never be absolutely positive that everyone who claims to have encountered authentic vampires are either naive fools or outrageous frauds; for surely in an infinite, eternal cosmos there is nothing imaginable—or unimaginable—which might not be true, somewhere or sometime.

The Adaptive Ultimate

Over the years the vampire myth has been a rich source of material for weird fiction writers, so it is perhaps not surprising that ever since the demise of the old-fashioned ghost story the vampire tale has become firmly established as the favorite fare of horror buffs the world over. But any hasty dismissal of such stories as merely escapist entertainment would, I suggest, be a mistake; for it is my contention that they also satisfy a primitive, age-old urge in the heart of every modern man or woman—the desire to experience the lost emotion of supernatural terror.

We may like to think of ourselves as being civilized, but beneath the thin veneer of modern culture there flows, deep as any subterranean stream, man's secret craving for the supernatural and the taboo; it is instilled in each of us by the timeless lore of the past, which no matter how sophisticated our lives may become continues to dominate our emotions and influence our minds. For though the terrors of the Ancient World have long been outlawed and set down as products of the unbridled imaginations of our ignorant forebears, the ingrained, atavistic need for the stark, purgative stimulation of supernatural terror has not—nor ever will be—winkled out from its impregnable stronghold in the dark chamber of the unconscious. And it is through the vampire story—in particular those that deal with deep-rooted fears and events which appear to violate natural laws—that we of the technological age can regain, albeit vicariously, that delicious excitement of spine-chilling horror.

Even so, it is only the more perceptive student of the horror story who fully appreciates the amazing scope of the vampire theme; for in the minds of the unenlightened public the word "vampire"only seems to conjure up the stereotyped image of Count Dracula, or some fang-toothed actor in a horror movie. Likewise, many habitual readers of horror fiction approach the theme with similar preconceived ideas, and are consequently inclined to denigrate vampire stories in the mistaken belief that they all revolve around the hoary old plot about an evil nobleman returning from the dead to ravish and suck the blood of beautiful virgins. However, despite its durable appeal, this antiquated concept is woefully out of date, and has, unfortunately, tended to obscure the fact that the vampire theme—far from being narrow and stilted— is extremely plastic, and has been productive of more variations than any other motif in weird fiction.

Ever since the great days of the pulp magazines in the 1930s, new images of the vampire have been constantly appearing in the pages of fiction, some surpassing even the wildest imaginings of our superstition-oriented ancestors. A strange assortment, they range from microscopic organisms to huge, world-destroying entities. Human vampires encountered in horror stories are also quite a heterogeneous bunch, ranging from the 10,000-year-old femme fatale in Robert E. Howard's *Conan the Conqueror* to the malevolent fetus in Eddy C. Bertin's *Circus of Darkness*. In between these two extremes are a wide variety of strange individuals whose special dietary requirements are often the only thing they have in common. On top of this, there are also stories about the vampirish activities of parts of the human anatomy, such as a severed hand, a woman's hair, and a man's eyes.

These days, with undead counts and countesses now considered passé, the traditional image of human bloodsuckers—as vicious, self-seeking predators—has undergone a dramatic change. In contemporary horror novels the prevailing trend is to portray vampires as highly intellectual beings living a separate but not entirely incompatible existence alongside the human race, with the pursuance of knowledge (rather than nubile maidens) as their main recreation.

Horror literature is also the natural habitat of a variety of animal vampires. Vampire bats still predominate, but some of the more innovative fantasy writers have bestowed vampirish tendencies on members of the

animal kingdom other than those traditionally associated with the
Undead, and have even transformed certain species of marine and insect
life into vampires.

Mother Nature, so often depicted as a kind and bounteous deity
by poets, also has her darker side. Perhaps there is even a hint of the
vampire in her ways, as the Marquis de Sade observed when he wrote:
"Nature hungers at all her pores for blood...out of death she kindles
life". Nowhere is this more evident than in those odd, out-of-the-way
places in remote, uninhabited areas of the countryside—like a secluded
meadow or a stagnant pool—which exude an air of malignancy bordering
on the vampiric. It is as though these sinister backwaters have an
indwelling personality—a *genius loci*—which is able, through some
mysterious process, to feed off the vitality of any sensitive person who
comes within its deadly aura.

The most exotic permutation of the vampire myth is undoubtedly
the anthropophagic or bloodsucking plant—though, to be honest, I doubt
very much if any such genus ever existed outside the pages of fiction.
Be that as it may, the obvious inspiration for these horticultural horrors
is that well-known curiosity of nature, the Venus -flytrap. This may
seem a rather innocuous source at first sight, but with Mother Nature
kindly giving the imaginative writer an inch, so to speak, he has craftily
taken the proverbial yard and dreamt up all manner of botanical
monstrosities, from blood-drinking blooms to man-eating trees.

The more grotesque specimens of vampiristic plant life—huge,
demoniacal growths resembling rooted serpents—are usually depicted
as plant-animal hybrids. Outwardly they are hideous travesties of
vegetable life, inwardly they are malefic carnivores with all the
aggressiveness and cunning of predators. Ever restless and sentient,
sometimes capable of limited movement, they capture their victims with
long frond-tentacles, devour them whole, and deposit the remains in
their capacious stomach sacs, there to be slowly digested.

Unchallenged as kings of the superphysical plant world are vampire
trees. The personification of vegetal malice, they are imbued with a
terrible, Satanic vitality, almost as though they were rooted in Hell itself.
Equally deadly—and equally fictional, I might add—are vampire vines.
To the more poetic fantasists they take on the likeness of wooden worms
vested with leaves, or, alternatively, tough leathery cordings transmuted
into a kind of pseudo-flesh. As flexible as rubber and capable of swift,
whip-like movements, they bind and choke the life out of their prey

in no time at all, draining out the life-blood through delicate shoots covered in minute suckers.

Conversely, blood-drinking flowers carry on the classical tradition of the beautiful vampire, but their beauty is merely a snare to attract unwary victims. For being fragile and more diminutive than their plant counterparts, and lacking the same freedom of movement, they overcome their victims by stunning them with a narcotic vapor, which enables the fanged blossoms to gorge themselves, unhampered, on the captive's blood.

The possession motif has also been successfully incorporated into stories about vampire plants. In such instances the human victim unwittingly eats the plant's seeds, which germinate inside him and, in due course, utilize his body as a plant pot; his blood providing the nutriment for the growing plant. Also quite common in both legend and fiction are plant deities. These are usually large, fantastically-shaped plants in which a demon has made its abode. Invariably they are worshipped as tribal gods and offered blood sacrifices to appease their wrath.

No inventory of the vampire's fictional guises would, of course, be complete without some reference to demonic vampires. Part of the world's mythology since records began, it was only natural that they would become founder members of horror fiction's gallery of monsters. And today, for obvious reasons, demonic vampires with insatiable sexual appetites are still popular with readers of lurid horror novels.

Perhaps the most unlikely manifestation of the vampire is one that is an extension or distortion of inanimate nature—for example, a stone with life-sapping potentialities. On the face of it this may seem an utter impossibility, but Frank Belknap Long, the popular fantasy author, gave a lot of people food for thought back in the 1930s when, through the medium of his novel *The Horror from the Hills,* he posed the question: "How do we know that stones cannot think; that the earth beneath our feet may not once have been endowed with a hideous intelligence?" He followed up this line of reasoning by suggesting the possible existence of a non-protoplasmic cycle of life of which we are completely unaware; one which antedates the process of biological evolution and is, even now, shaping inorganic matter into forms of primal malevolence.

Although it all seems highly unlikely, to say the least, it has not stopped other fantasy writers from extending the theme of active, malevolent life in objects that should be passive and inert. Taking their cue from Long, they have enriched weird fiction with fanciful tales about vampire-houses, blood-drinking statues, vampirous swords, and soul-stealing paintings. Other equally amazing variations on the traditional form include a vampiric brass rubbing, a chemical vampire, a bloodsucking postage stamp, and a vampire-song.

Vampires of fantasy fiction are not only found in divers forms, but also in many different locales. Apart from infesting the four corners of the earth, they are also in outer space, holding high carnival on the Moon and awaiting unwary space-travelers on Mars and Venus. Furthermore, they lurk in other dimensions, in the shadowlands of the dead, and in the magical realms of gods and demons. Literally—or rather literarily—speaking, they are everywhere imaginable.

To sum up, then, the vampire can be human or non-human, animate or inanimate, tangible or intangible, and it can dwell in a variety of places, both here on earth and in realms beyond the material plane of everyday cognizance. In short: the vampire has no fixed image and no fixed abode.

Taking all this into account, it is clear that the standard dictionary definition of the vampire is totally inadequate, and a much broader definition is required; one that can, in a few words, convey the common link between all members of the vampire fraternity—showing, for instance, what Count Dracula has in common with, say, a bloodsucking orchid. Therefore, having reached the conclusion that an all-embracing definition of the vampire must concentrate on motivation rather than outward form, I have formulated one as follows: A vampire is fundamentally a parasitic force or being, malevolent and self-seeking by nature, whose paramount desire is to absorb the life-force or ingest the vital fluids of a living organism in order to sate its perverse hunger and perpetuate its unnatural existence.

In putting forward this new definition of the vampire I am, of course, only too aware that I have attempted the impossible; for it is evident from the preceding inventory that the range of the vampire's guises is so staggering that even a definition as broad-based as this cannot cover them all. One is, after all, dealing with an incredible multi-monster, arguably the supreme creation of the fantasy writer's imagination.

Reference Works
The vampire superstition has, for centuries, attracted the attention

of mystics and scholars, and a considerable amount of information and theoretical discussion about this eternally fascinating subject can be found in the many books on occult phenomena that have been written since the late 16th century. The first major European vampire treatises were written by German academics in the early 18th century, and these were augmented midway through the same century by Dom Augustin Calmet's classic study, *Dissertations sur les Apparitions des Anges, des Demons et des Esprits, et sur les Revenants et Vampires*. A more succinct title, *The Phantom World*, was given to the first English translation in 1858. This book's value to modern students of vampirism can be gauged from the fact that extracts from it have appeared—verbatim or paraphrased— in most of the recent "popular" examinations of the vampire myth.

In the 19th century, many authorities on the occult touched upon the topic of vampirism in their writings, but apart from Collin de Plancy's *Histoire des Vampires* (1820) no major study was attempted. In contrast, the present century has produced an abundance of reference works. The earliest British treatises were A. Osborne Eaves' *Modern Vampirism: Its Dangers and How to Avoid Them* (1904) and Dudley Wright's *Vampires and Vampirism* (1914). Of little consequence, they were later eclipsed by Montague Summers' mammoth studies, *The Vampire: His Kith and Kin* (1928) and *The Vampire in Europe* (1929). Together these two scholarly tomes provide the most exhaustive survey of the European vampire tradition ever written, and will probably stand for all time as the definitive works on the subject. But, having paid them due tribute, one has to admit that for the average person they are likely to make very dull reading. What, in fact, tends to spoil them for non-academics is Summers' unfortunate habit of dwelling at great length on unimportant minutiae. Even in the valuable chapter on vampire literature, major prose works are omitted or hastily dismissed in favor of such trivia as vampire plays and operas, which are described at great length. Moreover, where less pedantic authorities might have contented themselves with a brief footnote, Summers wades in with full cast lists and superfluous details about the costumes worn by the actors. However, despite Summers' fondness for irrelevant data, it has to be said in his favor that his research has formed the backbone of all subsequent books on the vampire superstition.

In 1931, Ernest Jones supplemented Summers research with a brilliant study titled *On the Nightmare*. However, whereas Summers had written his books solely from the point of view of supernaturalism, Jones, a distinguished psychoanalyst, was primarily concerned with psychological explanations of the medieval superstition, in particular its connection with the nightmare. He concluded his findings by expressing the opinion that the vampire superstition was a result of man's unconscious and suppressed sexual feelings, of which the most prominent are repressed incestuous wishes and sensory perversions of infantile origin.

As one would expect of a leading occultist from the same era, Dion Fortune's classic study of occult pathology and criminality, *Psychic Self Defense* (1930), offers a vastly different interpretation of vampirism. Besides expressing a belief in the existence of vampires, the author warns her readers about the dangers of vampirish psychic attacks, and suggests methods of warding them off. Vampirism is also strongly featured in Rollo Ahmed's *The Black Art* (1936) and William Seabrook's *Witchcraft: Its Power in the World Today* (1940), though there is a marked difference of opinion between the two authors as to what constitutes a vampire. Ahmed, a prominent occultist of his day, naturally took for granted the veracity of the Undead, whilst Seabrook, an urbane world-traveler, makes it clear from the outset that he regards the legendary vampire as "ecclesiastic tommyrot"! Accordingly, he restricts himself to a recital of bestial acts performed by "real-life" vampires.

With the aforementioned authorities covering the ground so thoroughly, it was perhaps to be expected that many years would pass before another serious study of the vampire myth was attempted. In fact, it wasn't until 1962, when Ornella Volta brought out her controversial study *The Vampire*, that the file on the Undead was eventually reopened. Translated into English in 1965, this award-winning book examines, with a frankness only possible in recent years, the carnal side of vampirism in all it perverseness.

Volta's book having broken the ice, other studies of the vampire soon followed in its wake. On the Continent the French author, Tony Faivre, produced *Les Vampires* (1962), and his fellow countryman, Roland Villeneuve, gave double value with *Loups-garous et Vampires* (1963). Meanwhile, in the United States, Bernhardt J. Hurwood was introducing the vampire legend to a new generation of readers through three popular paperbacks, *Terror by Night* (Lancer, 1963), *Monsters and Nightmares*

(Belmont Books, 1967), and *Vampires, Werewolves and Ghouls* (Ace Books, 1968). All rely heavily on Summers' books for data, but at least their uncluttered prose makes them more palatable to the modern reader. The same comment applies equally to a book called *Horror!* (John Baker, 1967) by Drake Douglas, which examines, in an entertaining manner, the popular image of the vampire and other figures of terror associated with the horror film. At the turn of the decade, Douglas Hill published a book titled *Return from the Dead* (Macdonald, 1970), which claimed to be "The History of Ghosts, Vampires, Werewolves and Poltergeists." Disappointingly, it was not a patch on his earlier blockbuster *The Supernatural* (Aldus Books, 1965), which had a far better dissertation on vampires and werewolves in a chapter headed "Here Be Monsters."

The 1970s brought forth a bumper crop of vampire treatises. One of the best was *The Dracula Myth* (W. H. Allen, 1972), written by a Transylvanian-born author, Gabriel Ronay. Very readable, it traces the influential cult of the vampire from its origins in pagan lore and Christian ritual to its representation in modern horror films and literature. More derivative is Anthony Masters' all-encompassing study *The Natural History of the Vampire* (Rupert Hart-Davis, 1972), in which the author has supplemented his own research with lengthy quotes from Summers' treatises and other authoritative sources. Similar in format is Basil Copper's *The Vampire in Legend, Fact & Art* (Robert Hale, 1973), which claims to be "the most exhaustive popular study of the vampire ever published." It doesn't quite live up to its boast, but is, nevertheless, a useful guide for the uninitiated. Well laid out, the book examines the growth of the legend and its expression in literature, films, and the theatre, concluding with factual accounts of medical vampirism. More specialized is *The Vampire's Bedside Companion* (Leslie Frewin, 1975), by Peter Underwood, president of the Ghost Club. Highlights are an account of the alleged exorcism of the Highgate Vampire, which took place in 1970, and a contribution from Dr. Devendra Varma which presents a new theory on the genesis of Count Dracula

A more serious study from the same decade is Leonard Wolf's *A Dream of Dracula* (Little, Brown & Co., 1972). Described as a freely roving meditation on the vampire in legend, fact and fiction, it is noteworthy for a brilliant discussion of Stoker's *Dracula*. Equally absorbing is Reay Tannahill's history of the cannibal complex, *Flesh and Blood* (Stein & Day, 1975), which contains many references to vampirism. An even more scholarly work is Jan L. Perkowski's *Vampires of the Slavs* (Slavica

Publishers, 1976). The topics discoursed upon range from pre-Christian
Slavic mythology to vampire bats; and an excerpt from A. Osborne Eaves'
Modern Vampirism is also included.

Many references to vampirism are also to be found in the series
of books on magic by Kenneth Grant. In *The Magical Revival* (Frederick
Muller, 1972), psychic vampirism is dealt with in a chapter headed "Blood,
Vampirism, Death and Moon Magick." Elsewhere mention is made of
the Qliphoth, the world of shades or shells, which, according to Grant,
is inhabited by vampires and other sexually generated anti-powers. In
another of Grant's books, *Cults of the Shadow* (Frederick Muller, 1975),
he claims that sexual vampirism is rife nowadays owing to a breakdown
of moral codes. We are, he warns, attracting sexual demons from the
Qliphoth who absorb sexual radioactivity; and, if unchecked, this will
eventually pose a great threat to mankind. In much the same vein is
a book called *The Dark Gods* (Rider/Hutchinson & Co., 1980) by Anthony
Roberts and Geoff Gilbertson, which purports to reveal the true nature
of the evil forces at work in the universe. The authors claim that non-
corporeal entities from other dimensions have held this planet and all
its life-forms under a psychic siege for thousands of years. These malignant
ultraterrestrials, they say, have been known among mankind by many
graphically descriptive names, one of which is "vampire." Their main
aim, apparently, is to consume the energy of living beings, and have
chosen us because the eco-social systems on Earth form ideal "batteries"
from which they can draw their vital sustenance. Alternative explanations
for the "Dark Gods" phenomenon are also considered. One suggestion
put forward is that they are archetypal powers that channel and manifest
through the human collective unconscious; while elsewhere in the book
a possible link with the UFO phenomenon is discussed.

An obscure, crudely-written work that has aroused the curiosity of
bibliophiles due to its near-unobtainability is Stephen Kaplan's *In Pursuit
of Premature Gods and Contemporary Vampires* (1976). Published
privately by the Vampire Research Center in New York, its shortcomings
eventually led to its withdrawal. A later, more successful attempt by
Kaplan to set his parapsychological experiences down on paper is
Vampires Are (ETC Publications, 1983), for which he employed the
services of a ghost-writer.

Two contrasting studies from the 1980s are Bernhardt J. Hurwood's
Vampires (Quick Fox, 1981) and Olga Hoyt's *Lust for Blood: The
Consuming Story of Vampires* (Stein & Day, 1984). The former is a flashy

"coffee-table" book packed with photographs, essays, interviews, and trivia, all excitingly presented. It shouldn't be taken too seriously, however, as in some sections fiction is dressed up as fact. Ms. Hoyt's book, on the other hand, is a much more serious work; but unfortunately there is little in it that the informed reader will not have encountered elsewhere. The one exception is the chapter on contemporary vampires, much of which is compiled from the private files of Dr. Jeanne Youngson, president of the The Count Dracula Fan Club.

Minor studies/surveys written with the younger reader in mind include *Vampires, Werewolves, and Other Demons* (Scholastic Book Services, 1972) by Bernhardt J. Hurwood; *Vampires and Other Ghosts* (Addison-Wesley Publishing Co., 1972) by Thomas G. Aylesworth; *Vampires* (Lippincott, 1973) by Nancy Garden; *The Story of Vampires* (McGraw-Hill Book Co., 1977) by Thomas G. Aylesworth; *Vampires* (Franklin Watts, 1977) by Elwood D. Baumann; *Vampires, Werewolves and Demons* (Usborne Publishing, 1979) by Lynn Myring; and *Be Your Own Vampire* (Condor Publishing Co., 1981) By Thomas G. Aylesworth.

A book that is regarded as having given a major boost to the resurgence of interest in vampirism in the early seventies is *In Search of Dracula* (New York Graphic Society, 1972) by Raymond T. McNally and Radu Florescu. Subtitled "A True History of Dracula and Vampire Legends," it traces the evolution of the Dracula legend from its origins in 15th-century Romania to its exploitation in literature and the cinema. Singled out as the "historical Dracula" is the obscure Walachian warlord, Vlad Tepes, whose life and times are given an even more thorough coverage in another impeccably researched volume by the same authors, *Dracula: A Biography of Vlad the Impaler, 1431-1476* (Hawthorn Books, 1973). A less-detailed biography of this legendary figure can be found in *Dracula Country* (Arthur Barker, 1977) by Andrew Mackenzie; and similar territory is explored in *A Night in Transylvania* (Grosset & Dunlap, 1976) by Kurt Brokaw, which is mainly a travelogue through Romania, with some notes on vampire folklore and a survey of vampire films and literature. Aimed at a more general readership are two mammoth collections of Dracula memorabilia, Donald F. Glut's *The Dracula Book* (Scarecrow Press, 1975) and Peter Haining's *The Dracula Scrapbook* (New English Library, 1976). Both contain a wide-ranging selection of illustrated material concerning Dracula books, plays, comics, records, movies, and other diversifications.

Bram Stoker, the man who started this thriving industry in the first place, has also been the subject of several books, the pioneer work being Harry Ludlam's *A Biography of Dracula: The Life Story of Bram Stoker* (Fireside Press, 1962). Well-researched, and compiled with the invaluable assistance of Stoker's son, and Hamilton Deane, the actor-manager who revived *Dracula* on the stage in the 1920s, it is the source used in all subsequent books on Stoker and his immortal creation. A more controversial account of Stoker's life and career can be found in Daniel Farson's *The Man Who Wrote Dracula* (Michael Joseph, 1975). Not a particularly memorable book, its main claim to fame is its revelations about Stoker's private life. Apparently, like many other eminent Victorians, he was not quite as respectable as his public image implied.

A book which claims to be the first in-depth critical study of Bram Stoker's many-faceted novel is Clive Leatherdale's *Dracula: The Novel & the Legend* (The Aquarian Press, 1985). In his detailed analysis, the author considers the folkloric and historical background of the novel, and describes the development of the vampire legend in Europe. He also provides a brief biographical account of Stoker himself and discusses the genesis of his most famous work. By far the most interesting part of this study offers five interpretative perspectives, in which the text of the novel is analysed in terms of its pervasive and powerful sexual symbolism, its Freudian overtones, its religious themes, its relationship to occult and literary myths, and its significance as a political and social allegory.

Devotees of Dracula have been further catered for in offbeat publications such as Jeanne Youngson's *Dracula Made Easy* (Carlton Press, 1978), Victor G. Ambrus' *Dracula (Everything You Always Wanted to Know, But Were Afraid to Ask)* (Oxford University Press, 1980), and *The Dracula Collection* (Octopus Books, 1981). This last is a portfolio of fantasy/horror art presented as a personal collection of Count Dracula; it is supported by text which describes the unnamed author's visit to Castle Dracula.

Historical surveys of vampire literature have appeared at regular intervals since the mid-seventies, but all have fallen well short of being comprehensive. Not only have the authors failed to take into account the vast body of vampire fiction produced since the 1920s, but have also failed to recognize that the vampire is a polymorphic creation with a host of incredibly dissimilar guises.

One of the earliest surveys of vampire fiction was Margaret L. Carter's *Shadow of a Shade: A Survey of Vampirism in Literature* (Gordon Press, 1975). A rare book nowadays, it contains a valuable checklist of nearly 350 tales which have appeared in English-language books and magazines, with the emphasis on British authors. Similar, but with the accent on vampire verse, is James B. Twitchell's *The Living Dead: A Study of the Vampire in Romantic Literature* (Duke University Press, 1981). Two European surveys that would benefit from an English translation are *Le Vampire dans la Littérature Anglo-Saxonne* (1985) by Jean Marigny, and *La Bibliographie de Dracula* (1986) by Jacques Finné. The first is in two thick volumes, amounting to a total of 880 pages; the second comprises a 92-page survey of vampire and werewolf fiction, plus 120 pages of bibliography.

One of the most comprehensive listings of vampiriana ever assembled is *Vampires Unearthed* (Garland Publishing, Inc., 1983), which is described as "The Complete Multi-media Vampire and Dracula Bibliography." Compiled by Martin V. Riccardo, president of The Vampire Studies Society, it provides a massive checklist of vampire literature, covering novels, short stories, anthologies, poetry, articles, comic books, and children's literature. There is also a comprehensive listing of vampire movies, plays, television shows, and records.

For those curious enough to take their obsession with vampires to the ultimate stage there are two similarly-titled pamphlets available. One is *How to Become a Vampire in 30 Days* (1979) by Monica Mobley; the other is *How to Become a Vampire in Six Easy Lessons* (1986) by Madeline X. I do not think, however, that one is supposed to take them too seriously.

For those who wish to delve further into the subject of vampirism, the following books also contain useful information: *Psychopathia Sexualis* (1886) by Richard von Krafft-Ebing (available in several modern editions, it includes several case histories of compulsive blood-drinkers); *Folk-lore and Folk-stories of Wales* (1909) by Marie Trevelyan (contains accounts of vampire-chairs and a vampire-bed); *Strange Monsters and Madmen* (Popular Library, 1969) by Warren Smith; *Vampirism: A Sexual Study* (Late-Hour Library/Phenix Publishers, 1969) by Philip Carden and Ken Mann; *Vampires, Zombies, and Monster Men* (Aldus Books, 1975) by Daniel Farson; *Lure of the Vampire* (The Count Dracula Fan Club, 1983) by Martin V. Riccardo; *The Alchemy of Immortality: Vampires and the Aristocracy of Blood* (Boleskine House, 1983) by Frater

PVN; *The Transitive Vampire: A Handbook of Grammar for the Innocent, the Eager and the Doomed* (Times Books, 1984) by Karen Elizabeth Gordon; *The Living and the Undead* (University of Illinois Press, 1985) by Gregory A. Waller; *Vampire or Blood Fetish: Three Case Histories* (The Count Dracula Fan Club, 1986) edited by Dr. Jeanne Youngson; and *The Origins of Dracula: The Background to Bram Stoker's Gothic Masterpiece* (William Kimber, 1987), edited by Clive Leatherdale.

Part Two
The Vampire Motif in Weird Literature

The Introduction of the Vampire Motif
into European Literature
The precise entry of the vampire motif into fiction is something one is not able to establish with any accuracy, for the simple reason that it is impossible to tell whether the vampire tales in classical literature are fables or are meant to be taken literally, so adroit were the ancient storytellers at welding fact and fiction into an inextricable fabric of fantasy. Similarly, the Icelandic Eddas and Teutonic sagas of the so-called Dark Ages, which sometimes mentioned vampires, are not really fiction in the true sense of the word. However, as every survey must have a starting point, I will stick my neck out and opt for an obscure Anglo-Saxon poem called *A Vampyre of the Fens*, written at the beginning of the eleventh century, as the vampire's probable debut in a work of pure imagination. After this humble start all trace of the theme in post-classical literature is lost until the appearance of Sir Thomas Malory's *Le Morte D'Arthur* in the 15th century. Even then the vampire content of this medieval romance is restricted to a single incident concerning the high-born lady of a castle whose life is sustained by endless dishfuls of virgins' blood. Then, once again, the theme went unexploited for a couple of centuries, though there was still the oral tradition of peasant folklore to keep the vampire legend extant throughout this period.

The permanent induction of the vampire motif into European literature came in the eighteenth century, following the considerable interest aroused in vampirism by the publication of a spate of learned treatises on the subject. Like most fantastic themes, vampirism first found extensive embodiment in poetry, and it is generally accepted that the poem which had the signal honor of introducing the motif into modern European literature was Heinrich Ossenfelder's "Der Vampir" (1748). A few decades later the theme attracted the attention of the literati with the publication of two seminal ballads, Bürger's "Lenore" (1773) and

Goethe's "The Bride of Corinth" (1797). The latter was derived from Phlegon's classical fable of the corpse-bride Philinnion, and in turn inspired several other versions of this timeless tale of love-after-death.

The only eighteenth-century prose works with a vampire element which are remembered today are the Marquis de Sade's *Juliette* (1791) and *Justine* (1796), both of which express the view that vampirism is a grotesque extension of the link between sadistic eroticism and bloodshed.

By the beginning of the nineteenth century, interest in the theme had spread to England, where, as on the Continent, it initially found expression in poetry. Works by major poets of the period which allude to vampirism include Robert Southey's epic ballad *Thalaba the Destroyer* (1801), Coleridge's "Christabel" (1816), and Keats' "La Belle Dame sans Merci" (1819).

For some inexplicable reason, the vampire was almost entirely absent from works of fiction written in the pure or high Gothic style. A rare exception is Johann Ludwig Tieck's "Wake Not the Dead" (circa 1800), in which a wealthy nobleman unwittingly swells the ranks of the Undead when he enlists the aid of a sorcerer to bring his deceased wife back to life. In a narrative that is unremittingly grim, the most memorable sequence is the one describing the resurrected woman's postmortem transformation:

> The art of the sorcerer had indeed bestowed upon Brunhilda an artificial life, and due nourishment had continued to support the restored body; yet, this body was not able of itself to keep up the genial glow of vitality, and to nourish the flame whence springs all the affections and passions—whether of love or hate—for death had forever destroyed and withered it: all that Brunhilda now possessed was a chilled existence, colder than that of the snake. It was nevertheless necessary that she should love, and return with equal ardor the warm caresses of her spell-enthralled husband, to whose passion alone she was indebted for her renewed existence. It was necessary that a magic draught should animate the dull current in her veins, and awaken her to the glow of life and the flame of love; a potion of abomination— one not even to be named without a curse—human blood imbibed whilst yet warm from the veins of youth. This was the hellish drink for which she thirsted.
>
> Possessing no sympathy with the purer feelings of humanity, deriving no enjoyment from aught that interests in life and occupies its varied hours, her existence was a mere blank unless when in the arms of her paramour husband, and therefore it was that she craved incessantly after the horrible draught. Whenever she beheld some innocent child whose lovely face denoted the exuberance of infantine health and vigor, she would entice it by soothing words and fond caresses into her most secret apartment, where, lulling it to sleep in her arms, she would suck from its bosom the warm, purple tide of life.

This dark and sombre story, the moral of which is implicit in the title, was first rescued from obscurity by Charles Collins in his anthology *A Feast of Blood* (1967), and later anthologized by Peter Haining in *Great Tales of Terror from Europe and America* (1973), where it appeared as "The Bride of the Grave."

The Byronic Vampire

Tieck's story notwithstanding, at this early stage in the development of the vampire tale the female vampire was something of a rarity. Instead it was her male counterpart, in the guise of a cruel lover preying upon beautiful young virgins, who was to dominate the terror fiction of the early nineteenth century. The story that did more than any other to establish this trend was Dr. John William Polidori's "The Vampyre" (1819), which was considered quite sensational in its day because its vampire-hero was a nobleman. The real significance of this innovation was that ever since medieval times the vampire had been represented in folklore as an uncouth, disease-ridden peasant, and only with the publication of Polidori's story did the vampire acquire a romantic image. To quote Ornella Volta, "he became a fully rounded personage, acquiring the prestige of an archetype."

The enormous success of "The Vampyre" sparked off a host of crude imitations and plagiarised versions. On the Continent, where it was even more popular than in England, it underwent innumerable translations and even started a craze for vampire plays. Judged by today's standards, however, it is rather tame stuff, and any shock value it once possessed has evaporated with the passage of time. Nevertheless, as the forerunner of a whole host of vampire stories about bloodsucking counts and countesses, it deserves a honored place in the annals of vampire fiction.

When Polidori created his prototypal vampire, the misanthropic Lord Ruthven, he took as his model a real-life nobleman, the flamboyant Lord Byron, whom Polidori had ample opportunity to study as he was for a time his private secretary and traveling companion. Like his factual equivalent, the vampiric Ruthven takes a subtly perverse pleasure in tormenting those he loves; and it is this particular trait that identifies him as one of the many incarnations of the Fatal Man, the archetypal anti-hero created by the founders of the Romantic school of literature.

The Romantics were primarily obsessed with the affinity between love and death and the way pain is sometimes linked with pleasure. Accordingly, they portrayed the vampire as an irresistible seducer, the personification of darkness and forbidden desires. His choice of victims is almost exclusively limited to innocent young women, whom he takes a delight in corrupting, robbing them not only of their blood but also their virtue. Later, in the repressive Victorian era, when censorship and strict moral codes deterred authors from dealing specifically with certain human impulses, vampire stories were increasingly invested with erotic symbolism.

In appearance the Byronic vampire conforms to a stereotyped image. He is usually tall and gaunt with a leanness bordering on emaciation; his pale, spectral face is instinct with evil, and the terrible, demoniac eyes speak of a fathomless understanding of sin and passion—at times giving the impression that they can penetrate into the very heart of his victim and read her innermost thoughts. Another striking feature of the vampire's visage is the wide mouth with its thin, cruel lips of an unnaturally brilliant red, which, when curled back in anger reveal long, fang-like teeth. To complete the grimness of his aspect the bloodsucking peer is invariably dressed in funereal black; his long cloak flapping about him like huge bat-wings.

Paradoxically, despite the Byronic vampire's forbidding appearance, his female victims find him utterly irresistible. For though they may shrink instinctively from his presence at first, the fatal seducer's magnetic personality and overpowering sexual fascination overcomes their morbid fear of his ultimate objective. Using the stratagem of a lover rather than a predator, the vampire's initial amatory advances—feigned to lull his victim into a false sense of security—give no hint of the terror to come.

Feeding off the success of "The Vampyre", the obscure French author, Cyprien Bérard, wrote an unauthorized novel titled *Lord Ruthven ou les Vampires* (1820); and there are also Byronic overtones in some of Prosper Mérimée's sadistic vampire tales in *La Guzla* (1827). Contemporary with these, but showing the influence of Tieck rather than Polidori, is E. T. A. Hoffmann's "Cyprian's Story," one of twenty-nine interconnected stories in *The Serapion Brethren* (1818-1821). About a female vampire called Aurelia, this last was written despite the author's aversion to vampirism, which he once described as one of the blackest and most horrible ideas that can be imagined.

The most famous piece of vampiristry dating from the second quarter of the 19th century is undoubtedly Théophile Gautier's exquisite tale of love beyond the grave, "La Morte Amoureuse" (1836). The title refers to the beautiful courtesan Clarimonde, with whom a young priest,

Romuald, has become infatuated. After dying in mysterious circumstances she appears to Romuald one night and declares: "I have come a very long way, from a place from which no one has ever returned; and yet I am here, for love is stronger than death!" From that night onward the young priest leads a double life: by day he dutifully observes his vows; at night he carries on a passionate affair with his dreamland paramour. After three years of nocturnal debauchery Romuald shows no desire to exorcize his obsession, even though Clarimonde is sucking his blood to maintain her life-in-death existence; but an older priest who has discovered his guilty secret councils him otherwise. Bidding Romuald accompany him to the deserted cemetery where Clarimonde lies buried, he exhumes the body; and the moment he sprinkles it with holy water it crumbles into dust.

Several English translations of this much-anthologized story exist, each with a different title. They include "Clarimonde" (tr. Lafcadio Hearn), "The Dead Leman" (tr. G. Burnham Ives), "The Vampire" (tr. F. C. de Sumichrast), and "The Beautiful Vampire" (tr. Paul Hookham). The last two emphasize the vampire element more than the others, while Hearn's version comes the closest to capturing the emotional sensuality of the original.

Russian literature's first major contribution to the vampire canon was Gogol's "Viy" (1835). Grimly humorous rather than horrific, it concerns a young philosopher's fatal encounter with the king of the gnomes, whose name gives the story its curious title.

Poe and His Contemporaries

Meanwhile, in America, Edgar Allan Poe was turning out a string of masterly horror tales with morbid themes, several of which dealt with outré forms of vampirism. His undoubted masterpiece, "The Fall of the House of Usher" (1839), is, in my opinion, a classic example of the disguised vampire story. Dig beneath the Gothic trappings, ignore the side issue of premature burial, and what one finds is the real motif—psychic parasitism. The psychic vampire is, in fact, the ancestral home of the Usher family, and its victims are the current human occupants, Roderick Usher and his sister Madeline. The ancient, malevolent mansion—a sentient stone organism impregnated with the evil emanations of past generations of Ushers—is by some hideous process having a devitalizing effect on the doomed couple, bringing the horror of madness into their lives and condemning them, in true vampire fashion, to a living death.

Earlier, in "Ligeia" (1838), Poe had introduced into fiction the idea of mental vampirism, linking it with the allied theme of metempsychosis. The title character, a beautiful, highly intelligent woman, gradually withers away as the result of her husband's obsessive desire to know her completely—death occurring when he has absorbed all of her into his consciousness. Retribution for this subconscious act of vampirism follows when the dead woman's revenant possesses the body of her marital successor, bringing about a situation where the roles of victim and vampire are reversed.

Another story by Poe in which a man unwittingly vampirizes his wife is "The Oval Portrait" (1842). An artist totally absorbed in capturing an absolute likeness of his lovely young bride is unaware of the devitalizing effect it is having on her frail constitution. With each sitting her life-force ebbs further away, while the image on the canvas becomes more and more imbued with life, culminating in the model's death at the precise moment the painting is completed.

From a psychological viewpoint, these three stories may be interpreted as allegories of the author's own inner conflicts, particularly his guilt feelings about the death of the women he loved, who all seem to have wasted away while still young. In the case of Poe's mother his feelings of possessive love for her were, psychologically speaking, manifested in the subconscious desire to devour the beloved object. Such a form of love, psychoanalysts explain, is based on the desire—present in all of us to a degree—to become one with the beloved object by incorporating it. Even more intense were Poe's feelings towards his child-bride, Virginia, which were further complicated by the fact that she was his cousin, thus raising the bogey of incest. When she died of consumption at the age of twenty-one, the sight of the life gradually ebbing away from her frail body obviously left an indelible impression on Poe's sensitive mind, which later transposed itself into the pale, emaciated women of his stories, most of whom die unnaturally. The significant factor, however, is that they subsequently return from the dead, seeking revenge.

The real terror in Poe's stories lies in the anticipation of what may occur, not in the actual occurrence. For what is clear, once one has grasped the deeper significance behind these stories, is that what really tormented and finally drove Poe insane was the conviction that he was somehow responsible for the deaths of his loved ones, and feared some sort of retaliation for his "crimes" from beyond the grave, perhaps in the same fashion as he believed he had committed them—by a form of vampirism. But I doubt whether Poe ever contemplated the form of defense against such an eventuality as that carried out by the hero of "Berenice" (1833), who, motivated by similar fears, violates the grave of his deceased cousin in order to extract her dental weaponry, thereby rendering her impotent should she return from the grave as a thirst-raging vampire.

While Poe was opening up new avenues of exploration into the darker side of the human psyche with his subtle vampire tales, the majority of the world's fantasists were content to churn out traditional vampire yarns which relied heavily on outmoded Gothic effects. In England the vampire story sank to its lowest ebb with the publication, in 1845, of Smyth Upton's execrable short novel *The Last of the Vampires*. Hardly much better is the anonymously-written *Varney the Vampire; or, The Feast of Blood* (1847), which for many years enjoyed a reputation far greater than it deserved by virtue of its near-unobtainability and the laudatory remarks made about it by Montague Summers. However, since the publication of the 1972 Dover edition (reproduced from the pages of the magazine in which it originally appeared) it has been exposed as a dreary, rambling narrative written in the debased pseudo-Gothic style employed by the hack-writers of the "penny dreadfuls." Indeed, so crudely written is *Varney* that even the most unsophisticated member of today's reading public would reject it as pure drivel. The eponymous hero-villain—a camp version of the Byronic vampire—turns all those whose blood he sucks into vampires, undergoing various transformations in the process. After many adventures, Varney's sanguinary career finally ends when he commits suicide by leaping into the crater of Mount Vesuvius. Although the authorship of this novel was disputed for many years—Summers, for instance, favored Thomas Preskett Prest—it is generally accepted today that it is most likely the work of the Scottish writer James Malcolm Rymer.

Also rather disappointing by today's standards is the vampire episode from Alexandre Dumas' *The Thousand and One Phantoms* (1848), which usually bears the title "The Pale-faced Lady" when it is published separately. The only European vampire stories of any note to come from this comparatively barren period were those penned by a Russian author, Count Alexis Tolstoy. Produced between 1838 and 1847, they include "Amena," "The Vampire," "The Family of the Vourdalak," and "The

Reunion After Three Hundred Years." Hard to find today, they were last published collectively in *Vampires: Stories of the Supernatural* (Hawthorn Books, 1969).

In 1858 there appeared one of those not infrequent curiosities of English literature, *The Vampyre*, "by the Wife of a Medical Man." About the "Vampyre Inn," which preys on alcoholics, it is nothing more than a ludicrous temperance tract dealing with the evils of drink. In contrast, "The Mysterious Stranger," a short story translated from the German about 1860 for a book called *Odds & Ends*, is the genuine article. Set in Transylvania, and having such an unusual and eerie atmosphere as almost to challenge comparison with the masterwork of Bram Stoker, it has been suggested by some commentators that the villain of the story, Azzo von Klatka, was the model for Count Dracula.

The Vampire-Woman

With the emergence of the Decadent movement as an influential force in European literature in the late 1850s, macabre fiction at last showed signs of escaping from the strait-jacket of Gothicism, though the direction it subsequently took was not a healthy one, leading ultimately into the more unsavory byways of sadism and eroticism.

The horror stories of the Decadents are sophisticated and stylized, but display a morbid obsession with death and corruption, with abnormalities of human thought and sexuality, and the exploitation of all possible sensations, especially those that Victorian society considered taboo. Morally the Decadents were most influenced by de Sade, whom they saw as a kindred spirit, but thematically they followed in the footsteps of Poe, dwelling on such topics as unnatural love and the terrors of the tomb.

They key figure in the early days of the movement was the French poet Charles-Pierre Baudelaire, whose notorious book of poems, *Flowers of Evil*, was the source and inspiration of innumerable literary works in the years following its publication. Inevitably, such a dazzling display of depravity and flamboyant sensationalism was destined to incur the wrath of the authorities, and as a result six of the most "offensive" poems were ordered to be excised from the book. Among these were "The Vampire" and "Metamorphoses of the Vampire." In the latter, Baudelaire imagines himself surrendering, masochistically, to the kisses of a fierce vampiress; and from this point in time, until Bram Stoker's *Dracula* redressed the balance, the Fatal Woman was to dominate the literary scene.

The Fatal Woman's deadliest incarnation was the vampire-woman. A female equivalent of the Byronic vampire, she was depicted as the embodiment of lust and evil incarnate in woman—an insatiable nymphomaniac whose sex desire knows no bounds, extending even beyond the grave. Gargiulo, an obscure writer of the Decadence, once described her as an amalgam of absolutes: absolute beauty, absolute instinct, absolute perverseness, and absolute seductiveness.

The typical vampire-woman is, like her male counterpart, a stock type. Possessing an unearthly beauty and oozing sex-appeal, she is the quintessence of glamour. The supernatural splendor of her appearance, however, is a deception, masking the wickedness of her true nature; for just as the elegant marble tomb discreetly hides the hideousness of corruption, so does the vampire-woman's lovely flesh conceal the putrescence of her soul. Beneath the thin veneer of charm she is ferocious, scornful and sadistic, intent only on gratifying her lust and luring young men to their destruction.

The features of the vampire-woman are fairly standard. She has large, lustrous eyes which speak of monstrous fantasies and sanguinary orgies, mirroring the soul of one who has learned the secrets of the tomb and conquered death. Her scarlet mouth, slightly too large, is athirst and amorous—like a venomous flower waiting to suck in its prey. Her nose, classical in contour, inhales the whole of life with a terrible voluptuousness, sniffing the smell of rottenness with delight as though it were a heady perfume. And, if she is true to type, her hair will be red, either groomed in an irredescent coiffure of repellent opulence, or worn loose and flowing in a twining, serpentine profusion.

Despite her predatory nature, the vampire-woman's lovers find her irresistible, becoming as the proverbial fly in the spider's web. Even when her mask of pretense has been dropped to reveal the grim, hungry visage of a praying mantis, the victims enmeshed in the seductress's web of passion remain quite willing to barter the blood of their veins for her favors. Indeed, the novels of the Decadents teem with effeminate, submissive heroes who gain a masochistic pleasure from being the plaything of a cruel, dominant woman.

Of course, the femme fatale was not the invention of the Decadents, or even the Romantics—cruel, sensuous women with a penchant for destroying their lovers are to be found throughout the literature of

Antiquity and the Renaissance—but it was the Decadents, and later the Symbolists, who made her into an established type. So much so that by the turn of the century the "vamp" had become a cliché.

One of the most controversial studies of feminine evil is Algernon Swinburne's verse play *Chastelard* (1865), in which Mary, Queen of Scots is depicted as a vampiress whose fabled beauty is preserved by the spilling of her lovers' blood. At one point in the drama she voices her feelings thus:

> For all Christ's work this Venus is not quelled,
> But reddens at the mouth with the blood of men,
> Sucking between small teeth the sap o' the veins,
> Dabbling with death her little tender lips...

In *Les Chants de Maldoror* (1868), a collection of prose-poems by the Decadent author Le Comte de Lautréamont, we find at least one male vampire of the period who can hold his own with the aforementioned vampire-women. He is a sadistic, Byronesque figure called Maldoror, who, when not abandoning himself to depraved fantasies from the depths of his mind, delights in drinking children's blood.

The Golden Age

As well as the slightly scandalous contributions to the vampire canon made by Decadent authors during the mid-Victorian era, several pieces of vampiristry of a less sensational nature also appeared. These included "Phantoms" (1864), a lyrical prose-poem by Ivan Turgenev in which the narrator is taken for nocturnal rides through the sky by a beautiful Russian vampiress; "The Last Lords of Gardonal" (1867) by William Gilbert, in which a wicked nobleman enlists the aid of a wizard to bring a comely peasant-girl he has unintentionally murdered back to life— but wishes he hadn't when she is resurrected as a vampire; *Vikram and the Vampire; or Tales of Hindu Devilry* (1870), a collection of Indian folk-tales edited by Sir Richard Burton; *The Vampire City* (1875), a haunting novel by Paul Féval; and *Ye Vampyres!* (1877) by "The Spectre", a romanticized tirade against the evils of gambling.

Dwarfing all these, however, is Joseph Sheridan Le Fanu's "Carmilla" (1871), which is indisputably the greatest vampire story written prior to Stoker's *Dracula*. In this innovative novella and his other masterpiece, "Green Tea," Le Fanu, an eccentric Irish recluse, pioneered the psychological ghost story and also introduced the psychic sleuth into fiction. Like many other geniuses in the horror field, it is reported that his nightmares provided the inspiration for many of his stories, which were written by candlelight in the dead of night.

A theme which recurs throughout Le Fanu's work is that of abnormal love; and while "Green Tea" is about sex denied, "Carmilla" concerns an illicit relationship between two members of the same sex. In fact, the use of the "Horrid Mystery" setting is just an attempt to camouflage the real theme of lesbianism; for stripped of its Gothic trappings the plot of "Carmilla" is seen to revolve around a beautiful female vampire's attempts to seduce a frail young girl, and the supernatural connotation of the act of vampirism only predominates at the very end of the story.

Carmilla, the dominant partner of this strange liaison, is, unlike most fictional vampires, not without feelings of tenderness for her victim. During nocturnal visits to her reluctant lover she tries to placate her with these soothing words:

> Dearest, your little heart is wounded; think me not cruel because I obey the irresistible law of my strength and weakness; if your heart is wounded, my wild heart bleeds with yours. In the rapture of my enormous humiliation I live in your warm life, and you shall die—die, sweetly die, into mine. I cannot help it; as I draw near to you, you in turn will draw near to others, and learn the rapture of that cruelty which is yet love.

At first, pleasurable excitement is aroused in the young victim, gradually to be mingled with fear and disgust as the stranger's attentions become more intimate, more demanding. In comparison with these sequences, the story's supernatural resolution seems rather contrived, but it fails to dilute the impact of this superb narrative, which was, from a psychological viewpoint, way ahead of its time.

In the 1880s, when the Decadence was in its heyday, vampirism was a very popular motif in French "underground" literature, where it was mainly exploited for its sexual overtones. One of the minor French poets of the era, Maurice Rollinat, churned out a succession of ephemeral poems about femmes fatales, which for several seasons were all the rage in the Paris cafés. The source of inspiration for the frenzied poems in his *Névroses* (1883), such as "Le Succube" and "A la Circé Moderne", is, as in most of this author's output, the vampire-woman and the masochistic tendencies of her victims.

More durable in its appeal is Guy de Maupassant's classic story of an invisible vampire, "The Horla," which first sent shivers up and down the spines of the reading public in 1887. Told in the first person, the story's oppressive horror builds up gradually. At first the narrator has a strange feeling of being followed throughout the day by an unseen presence; then at night the Thing climbs on his bed, kneels on his chest, and grips his throat—

Last night I felt someone crouching on me, drinking my life from my lips, his mouth to mine. Yes, he sucked it from my throat like a leech! Then he arose, replete, and I awoke so bruised and shattered and exhausted that I was unable to stir.

Forever pursued by this invisible yet tangible being, the man feels himself being taken over body and soul by a force that will not be denied; it enters and governs him like another soul, a parasitic, tyrannical soul. But what are its ultimate intentions? The narrator has no doubts about that:

The Horla will make of man what we have made of the horse and the cow: his thing, his servant, and his food, by the mere force of his will.

In a last, desperate attempt to destroy the Horla, the pursued man locks it in a room and sets fire to the building, hoping in this way to rid the world of the menace let loose on it. But he soon begins to doubt the success of his wild scheme:

Suppose he was not dead...only time, perhaps, has power over the Invisible and Dreadful One.

Premature destruction? The source of all human terror! After man, the Horla—after man who can die any day, any hour, any moment, by every kind of accident, comes the Horla who can only die on his appointed day, hour, minute, then only because he has reached the limit of his existence!

No...no...there's no doubt about it, no doubt about it...he is not dead...and so I must kill *myself*!

It is a brilliant narrative, darkened by the same impending tragedy and preoccupation with the human miseries that overshadowed Maupassant's own life.

One of the most influential English vampire yarns of the 1880s was Phil Robinson's "The Man-eating Tree" (*Under the Punkah*, 1881). As the title suggests, it is about an anthropophagic tree with bloodsucking leaves, which the author poetically describes as "a great limb with a thousand clammy hands." This anomaly of nature, half breast, half plant, stands in the middle of a glade in central Africa, flourishing luxuriantly in a spot barren of all but the hardiest vegetation. In a memorable passage the story's narrator, the leader of a safari party, graphically describes the monstrous growth's reaction to his close proximity:

> The tree was quivering through every bough, muttering for blood, and helpless with rooted feet, yearning with every branch towards me. Each separate leaf was agitated and hungry. Like hands they fumbled together, their fleshy palms curling upon themselves and again unfolding, closing upon each other and falling apart again—thick, helpless, fingerless hands (rather lips or tongues than hands) dimpled closely with little cup-like hollows.

The safari leader approaches still closer, bringing about an even more violent response:

> It strained, shivered, rocked, and heaved. It flung itself about in despair. The boughs, tantalized to madness with the presence of flesh, were tossed to this side and to that, in the agony of a frantic desire. The leaves were wrung together as the hands of one driven to madness by sudden misery. I felt the vile dew spurting from the tense veins fall upon me. My clothes began to give out a strange odor. The ground I stood on glistened with animal juices.

The fearful vampire-tree is eventually blasted to pieces with an elephant gun, but not before it has devoured one of the native bearers, whose lifeless body is later retrieved from a huge stomach sac at the base of the tree, lying amid the half-digested remnants of other meals. Though not a classic by any means, this story has, nevertheless, a minor claim to fame as the forerunner of a whole host of stories about carnivorous plants.

In collaboration with his brothers, E. Kay and H. Perry Robinson, the same author penned two other unusual vampire yarns, One, "The Last of the Vampires," features a vampire-pterodactyl; the other, "Medusa," is about an alluring femme fatale who feeds on the life-force of her lovers, whom she subjugates by hypnotism. Both stories were originally printed in magazines in the 1880s, but later achieved hardcover publication in a collection titled *Tales by Three Brothers* (1902).

A slow-paced but well-crafted novella dating from 1887 is "A Mystery of the Campagna" by 'Von Degen' (a pseudonym used by Baroness Von Rabe, the elder sister of F. Marion Crawford). Set in Italy, it concerns the puzzling disappearance of a musician who has rented a villa just outside Rome. After making a determined effort to solve the mystery, his friends discover that he has become the victim of a centuries-old vampiress, whose sarcophagus is hidden away in an underground burial chamber. A similar fate almost befalls the hero of Julian Hawthorne's stylish novella "Ken's Mystery" (1888), in which a young artist touring Ireland falls in love with a legendary vampiress, and journeys with her into the past through the agency of a magic ring. Two other noteworthy stories from the same decade are Eliza Lynn Linton's "The Fate of Madame Cabanel" (1880), in which a beautiful young Englishwoman living among superstitious French peasants is brutally murdered after being mistaken for a vampire; and Frank Stockton's "A Borrowed Month" (1886), in which a young man suffering from a debilitating illness discovers that by the force of his will he can abstract energy and vitality from his companions. Psychic vampirism also forms the basis of two novels from the 1880s, Ivan Turgenev's *Clara Militch* (1882) and Edward Heron-Allen's *The Princess Daphne* (1888).

As might be expected from one of the most fertile periods in the history of supernatural fiction, the final decade of the nineteenth century yielded a rich harvest of vampire stories, many reflecting contemporary interests in diabolism, hypnotism, and new developments in psychology. Hypnotism, for example, plays an important part in "The Parasite" (1894), a superb novella by Arthur Conan Doyle, in which a frail, middle-aged spinster controls people's thoughts and actions from afar by her amazing mental powers. In particular, she conceives a passion for a university professor, whom she hypnotizes in an attempt to make him reciprocate her love. When this subterfuge fails she projects her soul into his body and makes him behave irrationally. As a consequence, not only is the professor's career ruined, but under the woman's parasitic influence he is compelled to rob a bank, and comes within an ace of mutilating his fiancée's features. At length the man's persecution ceases with the sudden death of his tormentor.

Another story which deals with an unusual form of mental vampirism is Vincent O'Sullivan's "Will" (1899). Reminiscent of Poe's stories in the same vein, it describes how a man with an irrational hatred for his wife relentlessly draws out and absorbs her life-force by gazing at her intently for hours on end. The woman's implacable will, however, survives her physical death, and from the grave she exerts a vampiric influence over her husband, until he, too, expires. The final irony is that soon after he has been interred beside his wife, voices are heard coming from within the vault. Perturbed by the dialogue between the dead couple—in which the man is heard to plead with the woman for his soul—the mourners break open the coffins to investigate, and find that the woman still has the appearance and warmth of one who has just died, but her husband's body is corrupt and hideous to behold, like a corpse that has rotted in its grave for years.

One of the most unconventional vampire stories ever written is "A Kiss of Judas," by 'X.L.,' which was originally published in *The Pall Mall Gazette* and later included in a collection of the author's stories titled *Aut Diabolus Aut Nihil* (1894). A "clubland adventure" with an uncharacteristically exotic flavor, it is based on the curious legend of the Children of Judas, the substance of which is that the lineal descendants of the arch-traitor are prowling about the world seeking to do harm, killing their chosen victims with one bite or kiss, which is so potent it drains the blood from their bodies at a single draught, leaving a wound on the poisoned flesh like three hideous scars in the shape of three X's, signifying the thirty pieces of silver paid to Christ's betrayer. The whole procedure is further complicated by the fact that, having chosen their victim, these malefactors must first commit suicide so that they can enlist the devil's assistance in their machinations. His part of the arrangement is to endow them with the power to return to the world of the living in any form they think best suited to obtain their objective. In this instance the villain of the piece, an evil-tempered man with a malformed face, chooses to return in the guise of a beautiful woman, thus providing a dramatic twist to the end of the story.

Equally odd—but for very different reasons—is Count Eric Stenbock's "A True Story of Vampire" (1894). About the wimpish Count Vardalek, who has a perverted passion for little boys, it is one of the few stories that feature a homosexual vampire of the male gender. The author of this otherwise mediocre story was a mad Russian nobleman domiciled in England, whose eccentricities included sleeping in a coffin and dining with a pet toad on his shoulder.

Traditional vampire stories with conventional plots were, of course, still being written. A typical example is the old-fashioned Gothic thriller "The Stone Chamber" (1899), by H. B. Marriott Watson. Guests at Marvyn Abbey, who stay the night in what was formerly the bedchamber of the notorious Sir Rupert Marvyn, awaken in the morning feeling exhausted and have red marks on their necks. The mystery is solved when the hero discovers a secret entrance to an underground burial vault containing the coffin of the undead knight.

Between the years 1898 and 1899, a leading British journal of the day, *Pearson's Magazine*, published a series of allegedly real ghost stories under the byline of E. & H. Heron (a pseudonym used by the mother-and-son writing team, Kate and Hesketh Prichard). Models of their kind, each story is an exploit of a psychic detective named Flaxman Low, whose services are enlisted to counteract the harmful activities of a motley assortment of occult phenomena. In "The Story of Baelbrow," for instance, he is called in to investigate mysterious deaths at a reputedly haunted house, and discovers that a previously ineffectual spirit-vampire has become a deadly killer by animating an Egyptian mummy, which the owner of the house has recently acquired for his private museum. Vampire-related phenomena are also encountered in "The Story of the Moor Road," in which a malevolent elemental becomes palpable after absorbing an invalid's vitality; and in "The Story of the Grey House," wherein guests staying at a secluded country mansion are strangled and drained of blood by a demoniacal creeper growing among the shrubbery.

Other noteworthy vampire stories to come out of this fruitful decade were "Old Aeson" (1891) by A. Quiller-Couch, "The Death of Halpin Frayser" (1893) by Ambrose Bierce, "The Fair Abigail" (1894) by Paul Heyse, "The Flowering of the Strange Orchid" (1895) by H. G. Wells, "Good Lady Ducayne" (1896) by Mary Braddon, "Let Loose" (1898) by Mary Cholmondeley, "The Woman With the Oily Eyes" (1899) by Dick Donovan, and "The Purple Terror" (1899) by Fred M. White. This last, another example of the carnivorous-plant story pioneered by Phil Robinson, concerns the fate of a group of explorers who are attacked by vampire vines in the Cuban jungle.

Vampire novels were also fairly common, but with one notable exception they were all routine commercial work. Who nowadays has ever heard of, let alone read, J. Maclaren Cobban's *Master of His Fate* (1890), Julien Gordon's *Vampires: Mademoiselle Reseda* (1891), or Mrs. Campbell Praed's *The Soul of Countess Adrian* (1891)? The same question may be asked of Prof. P. Jones' *The Probatim* (1895), Florence Marryat's *The Blood of the Vampire* (1897), H. Chaytor's *The Light of the Eye* (1897), and L. T. Meade's *The Desire of Men* (1899), none of which, in all probability, will ever be reprinted. The last two at least display a modicum of originality. Chaytor's novel, for instance, concerns a man whose eyes have the power to suck out people's vitality, while the forgotten potboiler by Meade revolves around weird experiments in a strange house, where the aged regain their lost youth at the expense of the young.

Count Dracula

All the vampire novels mentioned in this survey so far are, of course, overshadowed by Bram Stoker's immortal *Dracula*, which has been a phenomenal bestseller since it first appeared in 1897. Subsequent dramatizations for the stage and screen have added to its stature, until it has come to be regarded by all and sundry—horror buffs and the general public alike—as the epitomal vampire story. Though not without its flaws, this masterly portrayal of the fatal attractiveness of evil is undeniably the greatest and most influential vampire novel ever written; and despite changing tastes in horror fiction its popularity has never waned.

Primarily, the fascination of this undying classic is due to its highly sensational plot, but it is also noteworthy for two other reasons. Firstly it has systemized the rules of literary and cinematic vampirology for all time, and secondly we have in Count Dracula the definitive incarnation of the human bloodsucker.

Bram Stoker, a part-time author who had never written anything approaching a masterpiece before, chose a complex multi-narrative format for his *magnum opus*. This might well have spelled disaster for a writer of his limited ability, but in the event he carried it off brilliantly. The book's first four chapters consist of extracts from the journal of Jonathan Harker, in which the young English solicitor describes his eventful journey to the remote region of Transylvania to pay a visit on Count Dracula, with whom he is to arrange the purchase of property in England. Dracula's ancestral home is a half-ruined castle perched on top of the Carpathians, and it is during Harker's enforced stay in this forbidding edifice that his client's sinister nature is gradually revealed.

Today our impression of the Count—invariably portrayed in movies as a tall, handsome ladykiller—has become somewhat blurred, so to remind us of the original here is Stoker's description of his arch-villain:

His face was a strong—very strong—aquiline, with high bridge of the nose and peculiarly arched nostrils; with lofty domed forehead, and hair growing scantily round the temple, but profusely elsewhere. His eyebrows were very massive, almost meeting over the nose, and with bushy hair that seemed to curl in its own profusion. The mouth, so far as I could see it under the heavy moustache was fixed and rather cruel looking, with peculiarly sharp, white teeth; these protruded over the lips, whose remarkable ruddiness showed astonishing vitality in a man of his years. For the rest, his ears were pale and at the tops extremely pointed, the chin was broad and strong, and the cheeks firm though thin. The general effect was one of extraordinary pallor.

Hardly the suave image that Christopher Lee and others project on our movie screens, is it—more like the historical figure on whom Stoker is thought to have based his character: the merciless Walachian warlord, Vlad the Impaler.

Full realization that he has entered the lair of a vampire comes to Jonathan Harker after he ignores his host's warning not to leave his room at night. Having fallen asleep in a strange part of the castle, he awakens to find three seductive young ladies around him:

All three had brilliant white teeth, that shone like pearls against the ruby of their voluptuous lips...I felt in my heart a wicked, burning desire that they would kiss me with those red lips...They whispered together, and then they all three laughed—such a silvery, musical laugh, but as hard as though the sound never could have come through the softness of human lips. It was like the intolerable, tingling sweetness of water-glasses when played on by a cunning hand.

One was fair, with great wavy masses of golden hair and eyes like pale sapphires. She advanced and bent over me till I could feel the movement of her breath upon me. Sweet it was in one sense, honey-sweet, and sent the same tingling through the nerves as her voice, but with a bitterness underlying the sweet, a bitter offensiveness, as one smells in blood.

I was afraid to raise my eyelids, but looked out and saw perfectly under the lashes. The girl went on her knees, and bent over me, simply gloating. There was a deliberate voluptuousness which was both thrilling and repulsive, and as she arched her neck she actually licked her lips like an animal, till I could see in the moonlight the moisture shining on the scarlet lips and on the red tongue as it lapped the sharp white teeth.

Lower and lower went her head as the lips went below the range of my mouth and chin and seemed about to fasten on my throat. Then she paused, and I could hear the churning sound of her tongue as it licked her teeth and lips, and could feel the hot breath on my neck. Then the skin of my throat began to tingle as one's flesh does when the hand that is to tickle it approaches nearer—nearer. I could feel the soft, shivering touch of the lips on the super-sensitive skin of my throat, and the hard dents of two sharp teeth, just touching and pausing there. I closed my eyes in a languorous ecstasy and waited— waited with beating heart.

In the nick of time a furious Count Dracula bursts in upon the scene and commands the vampire-women to leave his guest alone, making it clearly understood that they can only satisfy their lust when *he* has done with him.

Some commentators have suggested that this lurid episode is based on the author's childhood experiences in a forbidding Victorian hospital, where the nurses duties included blood-letting; but I think it is more likely, considering the sweltering sexuality of the sequence, that it is based on Stoker's experiences in the London bordellos, which he allegedly frequented after his wife became frigid. In what was still a comparatively repressed era, scenes like this, with its rampant sexual symbolism, were rare in mainstream fiction of the day, and no doubt served to satisfy the sexual frustrations of quite a few of the book's male readers.

Although he remains "off-stage" for most of the time, Dracula is undoubtedly the dominant figure throughout the book. Egotistic and fiercely proud of his noble lineage, he is supremely confident of his power over ordinary mortals. His supernatural attributes, which make him such an implacable force of darkness, include the ability to metamorphose into a bat and, when the occasion demands, a thin, luminous mist. Also, like others of his ilk, he casts no shadow; nor is his image reflected in a mirror. Physically he is no less formidable, combining incredible strength with astonishing agility. In one memorable incident, observed by the imprisoned hero, Dracula emerges from a turret window in the wall of his castle and crawls, face downward, toward the abyss below; his cloak spread around him like great wings.

After being left in no doubt about the fate in store for him, Harker concludes that his only chance of salvation is to seek out the Count's resting-place during the hours of daylight and destroy him. In the event, he succeeds only in wounding the sleeping monster; and shortly afterwards the Count sails for London, where, amongst its teeming millions, he relishes the prospect of satiating his lust for blood and creating a new and ever-widening circle of disciples.

The novel's somewhat pedestrian middle section is presented in the form of letters, extracts from diaries, and transcriptions from phonograph recordings, all narrated by the central characters in the story. Initially they concern Dracula's arrival in England with his fifty earth-boxes, and the commencement of his nocturnal attacks on Lucy Westenra, who is progressively weakened to the point of death. The cause of Lucy's failing health is correctly diagnosed by Dr. Abraham Van Helsing, a Dutch physician versed in the occult; but despite his desperate efforts to save her—including numerous blood transfusions—the patient dies, only to return from the dead at a later date as a vampire. There then follows the harrowing ordeal of releasing the victim from the vampire's curse, in which the traditional method of staking is employed.

Dracula then turns his attentions to Mina Harker, whom he spiritually contaminates in a profane ritual involving a mutual exchange of blood. Determined to save her soul, Mina's friends, under the guidance of Van Helsing, track down the Count to his hiding-place in London, forcing him to abandon his plans to create a vampire colony in England. Dracula's ensuing flight back to his homeland, relentlessly pursued by Van Helsing and the others, makes an exciting climax to the story, which culminates in the King-Vampire's apprehension and final destruction before he can reach the sanctuary of his lair.

Although there is no reason to believe that Stoker regarded *Dracula* as anything other than a straightforward story of Good versus Evil, most commentators today interpret it as a sexual rather than a theological allegory, even going so far as to call it one of the most erotic novels ever written. Stoker, himself, always maintained that the genesis of his novel was a vivid nightmare; but following recent disclosures about his private life the book has taken on a new significance, and is now generally regarded as an expression of the author's frustrated sensuality.

Whether or not one accepts this interpretation, or, for that matter, any of the others that have been placed on this novel from time to time, there can be no disputing the fact that *Dracula* is a masterpiece in its own field; for like all those classic works of literature which give us a keener understanding of the forces of darkness it becomes part of the reader's experience, leaving an indelible impression upon his mind.

The Spawn of Dracula

By the beginning of the twentieth century the vampire story was securely established as a distinct and popular genre. Initially, quite a few of the stories produced were derived from *Dracula*, but as the century wore on an increasing number offered new and unusual variations on the theme.

A well-known turn-of-the-century vampire story which has been anthologized several times since its initial appearance in the December 1900 issue of *Pall Mall Magazine* is F. G. Loring's "The Tomb of Sarah." Based on established vampire lore, it chronicles the nocturnal activities of an undead witch, who is accidentally released from the confinement of her tomb when it is disturbed by workmen. For a while the vampire's nightly sorties in search of blood cause concern among the local community, but she is eventually trapped and permanently laid to rest by the time-honored ritual of driving a stake through her heart.

All but forgotten today are two minor stories about vampiric women, Hume Nisbet's "The Vampire Maid" and "The Old Portrait" (*Stories Weird and Wonderful*, 1900). Similarly neglected is Richard Marsh's ingenious story "The Mask" (*Marvels and Mysteries*, 1900), in which a homicidal madwoman adept in the art of mask-making transforms herself into a raving beauty and threatens to suck the blood of the hero. Basil Tozer's "The Vampire" (1902) has also sunk into oblivion; and the same fate might well have befallen Frank Norris' "Grettir at Thorhall-stead" (*Everybody's Magazine*, April 1903) had it not been rescued from an undeserved obscurity by fantasy historian Sam Moskowitz, who reprinted it in his splendid anthology of rediscovered masterpieces, *Horrors Unknown* (1971). An uncharacteristic piece by this American master of realism, it purports to be an episode in the life of the legendary Icelandic hero, Grettir; and is one of the few stories in which a vampire of the uncouth-peasant type is represented. Another outstanding story from this period by an American writer is Mary E. Wilkins-Freeman's "Luella Miller" (*The Wind in the Rose-bush & Other Stories of the Supernatural*, 1903), in which the theme of psychic vampirism is given a realistic treatment.

One of the finest British vampire tales from the Edwardian era is M. R. James' "Count Magnus", which has been anthologized many times since its introduction in *Ghost Stories of an Antiquary* (1904). Full of antiquarian erudition, yet written in a terse, economic style, it concerns an English traveler's discovery of suppressed legends about a long-dead Swedish nobleman, and relates the incidents leading up to the doomed man's gruesome demise at the hands of the undead Count and his hideous familiar.

A minor British author who shared James' ecclesiastical background was Sabine Baring-Gould. Among the supernatural tales collected in his *A Book of Ghosts* (1904) is a curious story titled "A Dead Finger," in which a man haunted by an animated finger is attacked vampirically when the rest of the body it belongs to materializes. Similarly, in Morley Roberts' "The Blood Fetish" (1909) a severed hand lives on as an independent entity by absorbing blood. On more traditional lines is "The Vampire Nemesis" by "Dolly," a trite yarn from 1905 about a suicide who is reincarnated as a vampire bat. Also from this period come Vincent O'Sullivan's "Verschoyle's House" (1907), which features a vampire tree, and Horacio Quiroga's "The Feather Pillow" (1907), in which a young woman has all the blood gradually sucked out of her body by a monstrous insect secreted in the pillow on her bed. Even more sensational is F. H. Power's "The Electric Vampire" (*London Magazine*, October 1910), in which a mad scientist creates a giant, electrically-charged insect that feeds, vampirically, on human blood.

On the Continent, in the early 1900s, traditional horror stories with their outmoded Gothic paraphernalia were being superseded by those with a more naturalistic treatment. Exemplifying this shift away from the supernatural is the short story "A Vampire" (1907) by the Italian author Luigi Capuana, whose realistic style often makes it read more like an impersonal case history than a tale of terror. The few vampire novels produced during the Edwardian era have little to commend in them. *A Vampire of Souls* (1904) by "H.M.P." has been described by Montague Summers as "a semi-apocalyptical novel of little value"; and *The Woman in Black* (1906) by M. Y. Halidom and *The House of the Vampire* (1907) by George Sylvester Viereck are similarly undistinguished, although the latter has a certain curiosity value. About a famous author who absorbs ideas from young men by a form of mental vampirism, it was probably meant to be a satirical dig at Oscar Wilde.

By the beginning of the second decade of the twentieth century the golden age of supernatural fiction was drawing to a close, but a few quality stories continued to appear, among them some fine vampire tales. Connoisseurs of the genre will need no introduction to F. Marion Crawford's "For the Blood is the Life" (1911) and E. F. Benson's "The Room in the Tower" (1912), whose repeated printings have elevated them to classic status. Crawford's piece, set rather unusually in a warm Italian locale, is a sad little tale of unrequited love, in which an attractive gypsy girl returns from the dead to vampirize the young man who has spurned her. In contrast, the vampiress in Benson's story is old and withered, and does her haunting dressed in a rotting shroud. The vampiric revenant of a suicide, she is first encountered by the hero in his nightmares, which are subsequently fulfilled when he visits the home of an old school-friend and spends the night in the haunted room in the tower. In the dead of night a peal of thunder wakes him from his sleep, and the accompanying flash of lightning reveals the old woman of his dreams leaning over the end of his bed, watching him intently. Slowly the ghostly apparition draws nearer, places a hand on the side of the young man's neck, and whispers these chilling words in his ear: "I knew you would come. I have been long waiting for you. Tonight I shall feast; before long we will feast together!"

Another leading exponent of the horror story in the first half of the twentieth century was Algernon Blackwood. Described by H. P. Lovecraft as "the one absolute and unquestioned master of weird atmosphere," he specialized in stories about the mysterious, hidden aspects of nature. In his best uncanny tales the indefinable atmosphere of a landscape often materializes into individual entities gifted with thought and a will of their own. Whether it be the nature-spirit of a snow-clad mountain, a river, or a forest, each has an intense and aggressive personality that borders on the vampiric, so that any sensitive person who falls under their spell is liable to become drained of his life-force. An extreme example of this is the short story "A Descent into Egypt" (1914), in which the spirit of Ancient Egypt absorbs a man's personality until there is nothing left of him but a human shell.

One of Blackwood's most popular "nature" stories is "The Transfer" (*Pan's Garden*, 1912), which pits against each other two highly contrasted vampires—one human, the other topographical. Mr. Frene, the human adversary in this extraordinary contest is described as "a great human sponge, crammed and soaked with the life he had absorbed—stolen— from others." Unconsciously, he vampirizes everyone with whom he comes in contact, draining them of their vitality, their ideas, even their very words. Thus in a crowd he grows vital from sucking in all the loose energy around him; alone, he droops and languishes. In startling contrast, the topographical vampire—referred to in the story as "the Forbidden Corner"—is a barren patch of land in an otherwise luxuriant garden. Stronger than Mr. Frene, it exerts its strange, hypnotic power to draw him within its center, and absorbs all the vitality he has appropriated from others, transforming itself in the process into a thriving mass of vegetation, and leaving its victim a spent force from that day on.

A pioneer of the modern psycho-sexual image of the vampire in the early days of this century was the German author Hanns Heinz Ewers, whose Nazi sympathies have, understandably, caused his work to become neglected since the Hitlerian war. Ewers' most sensational contribution to the vampire canon is *Alraune* (1911), the second of three novels featuring his anti-hero, Frank Braun. After hearing a fascinating account of the medieval superstition relating to the mandrake root (called *alraune* in Germany), Braun persuades his uncle, Professor Jacob ten Brinken, to use his biologic knowledge to create a modern counterpart of the evil mannikin. Accepting his nephew's challenge, the professor embarks on a blasphemous experiment: artificially inseminating the most shameless whore in Berlin with the semen of a vicious sex murderer, he eventually produces a pseudo-being of the female gender, who he names Alraune after the root-creature that had suggested her creation. Brought up as the professor's ward, she matures into a beautiful but soulless woman, who brings disaster to every man who falls under her spell. Braun, too, eventually succumbs to Alraune's sexual allure, and finds he hasn't the strength or desire to resist when she starts sucking his blood. Fortuitously, he is saved from serious harm when Alraune plunges to her death while sleepwalking.

In 1912, Bram Stoker ostensibly returned to the vampire theme in his novel *The Lady of the Shroud*, but those readers hoping for another *Dracula* must have been very disappointed to find it contained only a fake vampire element. In other respects, too, the novel is sadly lacking when compared with this author's *magnum opus*. A shorter piece by Stoker, "Dracula's Guest," originally published in 1914 in a posthumous collection titled *Dracula's Guest & Other Weird Stories*, is also something of a let-down. Not written as a short story in the first place, it is actually a sequence which was cut from the final draft of *Dracula*; and the Count's failure to make an appearance throughout the entire narrative makes it doubly disappointing.

Other minor pieces of vampiristry from this decade are Reginald Hodder's novel *The Vampire* (1913), in which the female leader of an occult fraternity resorts to psychic vampirism to replenish her waning vitality; George Soulie's translation of a Chinese folktale, "The Corpse the Blood-drinker" (*Strange Stories from the Lodge of Leisures*, 1913); Alice and Claude Askew's "The Vampire" (1914); Bernard Capes' "The Mask" (*The Fabulists*, 1915), which concerns a vampiric portrait; Mrs. Stanley Wrench's "The Vampire" (1915); Amelie Rives' *The Ghost Garden* (1918), in which the vampiric ghost of a dead woman draws the hero into her power and drains his vitality; and M. R. James' ecclesiastical vampire tale, "An Episode of Cathedral History" (*A Thin Ghost & Others*, 1919).

The much-loved American fantasist, A. Merritt, rarely touched upon the subject of vampirism, but when he did the results were always memorable. In his famous lost-race novel *The Moon Pool* (1919), for instance, there is an incredible entity called the Shining One, which represents the ultimate in vampiric development. A whirling, shimmering ball of living light, with seven globes of seven colors shining above its glowing core, it dwells in a hidden world beneath the Pacific ocean, which is linked to the surface by a doorway located in ancient ruins on the island of Nan-Tanach. Luring human victims through the portal, it enfolds them in its fiery embrace, drawing their life-force into and through itself; in its place it sets its own brand of life, infusing its desires, memories, and will, until its victims—on whose faces alternates a look of rapture and horror—are mere shells through which it gleams. Afterwards they join the monster-god's slave-army of living dead, becoming, in effect, an extension of its personality. It all adds up— as Merritt put it himself—to vampirism inconceivable.

A fast-paced, tremendously thrilling occult novel which has remained popular for over seventy years is Sax Rohmer's *Brood of the Witch-Queen* (1918). In part of the narrative subservient to the main plot there is a memorable sequence where the young heir to the House of Dhoon, the future Lord Lashmore, is taken to a secret underground cell and shown the partially-preserved body of his ancestor, Paul Dhoon:

> Yellow and seared it was, and his joints protruded through it, but his features were yet recognizable—horribly, dreadfully, recognizable. His black hair was like a mane, long and matted, his eyebrows were incredibly heavy and his lashes overhung his cheekbones. The nails of his fingers...no! I will spare you! But his teeth, his ivory gleaming teeth— with the two wolf-fangs fully revealed by that death-grin!...
>
> An aspen stake was driven through his breast, pinning him to the earthen floor, and there he lay in the agonized attitude of one who had died by such awful means. Yet—that stake was not driven through his unhallowed body until a whole year after his death!

From that day on the young man has to live with the terrible knowledge that in his veins runs the tainted blood of a vampire. This vile strain, he learns, has come down from a 17th-century ancestress, Mirza, wife of the fourth baron, who met a violent end when her husband ordered her to be decapitated for practicing the Black Arts. Her spirit, however, has remained earthbound, forced by a deathless, unnatural longing to seek incarnation in the body of a living person—a desire that is eventually gratified when her revenant possesses the body of the current Lady Lashmore, and uses her as an instrument of revenge.

Another exciting novel by Sax Rohmer, *Grey Face* (1924), has many of the trappings of the bizarre crime thrillers with which he made his name, but is of more interest than usual because of its original variation

SSCT

on the vampire theme. Ostensibly it is a murder mystery in which a series of gruesome murders are perpetrated by a phantom killer with a grotesque spectral countenance; but the motive behind the crimes is weird enough for a horror story. The elusive Grey Face, as the murderer is dubbed, remains in the background for most of the narrative, and the dominant character is a man called Trepniak, who, with his handsome looks and brilliant mind, has gained a circle of admirers among London's wealthy Park Lane Set. Trepniak, however, is not all he seems, for instead of being in his prime, as his appearance suggests, he is considerably older. In due course it comes to light that he is an unethical scientist who has found a means to make himself immortal by using a system of rejuvenation based on the discovery of the amazing properties of a certain gland in the human body, an extract from which, when mixed with blood, makes a serum with the power to endow the user with perpetual youth and vigor. The only drawback is that if the user is deprived of the serum for any length of time he returns to his true age and his face becomes deathly grey and cadaverous—the very same image that had imprinted itself upon the minds of the phantom killer's dying victims. For that is the surprise revelation reserved for the final act in the drama— Trepniak and Grey Face are one and the same!

The End of an Era

One of the prime weavers of vampire yarns in the 1920s was E. F. Benson, whose noted collection of short stories, *Visible and Invisible* (1923), contains those two memorable incursions into the nightmare world of the vampire, "Mrs. Amworth" and "Negotium Perambulans." In the former, a middle-aged woman residing in a sleepy English village appears to be a nice, friendly person by day, but at night she turns into a vicious, blood-seeking vampire; and, in the latter, an avenging angel in the repulsive guise of a huge slug violently attacks and sucks the blood of two men who have committed sacrilege. No less terrifying is the supernatural manifestation in Benson's other major vampire tale of the decade, "And No Bird Sings" (*Spook Stories*, 1928). Here the vampirizing is done by a malicious elemental, which assumes the hideous form of a giant phosphorescent leech.

In 1927 the Czech author Jan Neruda had his well-known short story "The Vampire" published in the omnibus volume *Great Short Stories of the World*. About a young artist nicknamed "The Vampire," because his subjects—all sickly people—die after he has painted them, it hardly deserves the accolade of "great", and its neat, if rather morbid twist on the vampire theme owes too much to Poe's "The Oval Portrait" for it to be classed as original. Ironically, the most recent reprinting of this story was in *The Dracula Book of Great Vampire Stories*, thereby devaluing the word "great" for a second time. Other vampire stories from the twenties that are occasionally reprinted include Jean Ray's "The Cemetery Watchman" (*Les Contes du Whisky*, 1925), Dion Fortune's "Blood-lust" (*The Secrets of Dr. Taverner*, 1926), and Edith Wharton's "Bewitched" (*Here & Beyond*, 1926). Almost forgotten, however, is Uel Key's "The Broken Fang" (*The Broken Fang and Other Experiences of a Specialist in Spooks*, 1920), a fanciful slice of hokum in which murder victims are drained of blood and turned into vampiric zombies. Another "lost" story is Lavinia Leitch's "A Vampire," which made its first—and apparently last—appearance in *A Vampire & Other Stories* (1927).

Out of all the vampire novels published in the 1920s, by far the most innovative was H. H. Ewers' *Vampire* (1922), which, by treating vampirism as a psycho-sexual perversion, went further than any other novel of its day in divesting the vampire theme of its supernatural connotation. The hero, Frank Braun, after narrowly escaping death at the hands of Alraune, makes his way to America, arriving there at the outbreak of the war in Europe. On a tour to raise funds for the Kaiser's cause, he is suddenly stricken with a mysterious, undiagnosable malady, which leaves him feeling weak and dizzy. Inexplicably, the condition is temporarily alleviated while he is in the company of an old flame, Lotte Van Ness, but afflicts him again when circumstances keep them apart. Adding to his confusion is the fact that all the other women he makes love to desert him immediately afterwards, often hinting before they leave that there is something loathsome about him. The mystery is finally solved when Lotte reveals that Braun's periods of recovery were due to acts of vampirism on his part, committed in a state of trance during their lovemaking. Deeply in love with Braun, Lotte had not turned from him in disgust like his other girlfriends, but willingly allowed small quantities of her blood to be drained, even though it irreparably damaged her health.

A similar vampire-victim relationship occurs in Dion Fortune's occult novel *The Demon Lover* (1927). The heroine, a mediumistic young woman named Veronica Mainwaring, unwittingly strays down the Left-Hand path of magic when she comes under the corrupting influence of Justin Lucas, a rebellious member of an occult society. After discovering that they had been lovers in a previous incarnation, she is persuaded to participate in his illicit experiments in astral projection, in which her astral form is sent on missions to steal secrets from Lucas' fellow occultists. At length, Lucas' treachery is exposed, and rather than face the wrath of the Brotherhood he vacates his physical shell and seeks refuge on the astral plane. Pronounced medically dead, his lifeless body is duly buried; but Veronica soon discovers that her lover's personality continues to exist.

At first the rebel occultist's disembodied ego is unable to materialize properly, but by drawing vitality from Veronica achieves an initial manifestation as a sheeted ghost. In time, Lucas' earthbound spirit gets strong enough to possess the body of a dog, through which it commits minor acts of vampirism. However, when the dog is killed a new host has to be found, for without any physical organs that can draw energy from the animal and vegetable kingdoms by the process of ingestion and digestion, a spirit-vampire has to find its supply ready-made. Consequently a life of vampirism is forced on the rebel, until Veronica persuades the Brotherhood to give him a second chance; and at a conciliatory meeting with the leader of the occultists, Lucas agrees to make atonement for his duplicity. The price he has to pay, however, is a harsh one. After a ceremony is performed to reanimate his exhumed body, he finds that he has been denied a full recovery, and must live out the rest of his days a sightless invalid.

Several routine thrillers with a vampire motif appeared in the 1920s. These included M. C. Sawbridge's *The Vampire* (1920), Henry Carew's *The Vampires of the Andes* (1925), Gertrude Dunn's *The Mark of the Bat* (1928), and Claude Farrere's *The House of the Secret* (1928). In this last, two residents of an old French chateau have lived to great ages through consuming the blood and flesh of youth.

The prolific British mystery writer, Sydney Horler, occasionally strayed into the horror field, as evidenced by his vampire novel *The Curse of Doone* (1928); but its dated dialogue and "women's magazine" style are hardly guaranteed to endear it to modern readers. In fact, the low standard of British horror novels in the late twenties was indicative of a decline in that nation's traditional expertise in fashioning tales of terror and mystery; and it was left to a talented bunch of writers from the New World to give the horror genre a much-needed shot in the arm.

New Blood

The sudden eruption of American virtuosity in a literary subgenre which had always been considered the main preserve of European writers was almost entirely due to one tradition-shattering event—the advent in the United States of the first all-fantasy magazine in the world, the now-legendary *Weird Tales*. Founded in March 1923, this immensely influential publication pioneered the development of the weird-fantasy story as a specialized form of popular fiction, and cradled many of fantasy literature's greatest exponents.

Printed on cheap wood pulp paper, with garish, brightly colored covers to catch the eye of newsstand browsers, *Weird Tales* was a superior specimen of the often-derided pulp magazines, which in the years between the two world wars provided low-priced entertainment for millions of Americans. During its thirty-year life span "The Unique Magazine," as it was subtitled, published an amazing variety of fiction, from old-fashioned tales of Gothic horror to futuristic weird-scientific yarns. As was only to be expected, out of the many themes exploited none were more popular than vampirism; and over the years literally hundreds of vampire stories, featuring every conceivable kind of vampiric manifestation, appeared in the magazine's pages. A great many, it must be conceded, were fairly routine, but some were among the best ever written.

The author most closely associated with *Weird Tales'* formative years is the enigmatic H. P. Lovecraft, who, despite being denied critical recognition during his lifetime, is today generally regarded as one of the greatest writers of horror fiction the United States has ever produced. One of the first vampire tales *Weird Tales* published was his "The Hound" (February 1924), in which an undead sorcerer wreaks a terrible vengeance on two thrill-seeking grave-robbers who rifle his tomb. Like much of Lovecraft's early work it wallowed in purple prose and Poe-esque rhetoric, but there was, nevertheless, something compelling beneath the sensationalism.

August Derleth, a correspondent and devoted admirer of Lovecraft, made his debut in *Weird Tales* at the age of seventeen with an extremely naive yarn called "Bat's Belfry" (May 1926), which deservedly received a cool reception from the magazine's readers. Undaunted, the precocious teenager went on to churn out a further twenty-four prosaic supernatural vignettes for "The Unique Magazine" in the 1920s, including another two vampire tales, "The Coffin of Lissa" (October 1926) and "The Tenant" (March 1928).

A featured story in the February 1925 issue was Victor Rowan's "Four Wooden Stakes." About a whole family falling victim, one by one, to the curse of vampirism, it has failed to stand the test of time and seems very dated today. In contrast, Everil Worrell's "The Canal" from the December 1927 issue has a timeless quality about it. A haunting tale of a young man's infatuation for a mysterious vampiress who lives on a barge, it evokes with singular subtlety yet seeming simplicity a sense of genuine weirdness.

A far-fetched but ingenious story in the same issue, "The Devils of Po Sung" by Bassett Morgan, tells of a fabulous lagoon in South America, which is guarded by huge vampire-orchids planted in human carcasses. Repulsively flexible to the touch, the scarlet, anesthetic-throated flowers wrap themselves around their victims and suck them dry of blood. Contrary to the norm, the terrible orchids bloom at night and close up when the sun shines—a nice touch by the author, linking them with the human vampire's inverted life style.

A personal favorite among the roster of vampire stories from *Weird Tales'* early issues is H. F. Scotten's "The Thing in the House" (May 1929). A pseudo-scientific thrill-tale, it features an invisible thought-vampire, the creation of a deranged professor who believes he has discovered the secret of life. His startling theory is that in a hidden compartment of the brain lies a bit of radioactive mineral which produces life by bombarding the atoms of the body with a constant stream of electrons, causing vibrations which activate the human machine. The crux of his theory, however, is that after death the electrons are thrown off from the lode in the brain and journey on an inconceivable orbit through space, eventually fusing together into a new mass, which resumes its function of producing life-giving vibrations in a human embryo.

After discovering that the flight of these electrons can be temporarily arrested and controlled by intense cerebral concentration, the professor, who has a taste for tales of terror, conceives the foolhardy idea of fashioning them into a thought-creature: a hybrid of Bierce's "The Damned Thing," Crawford's noxious horror from "The Upper Berth," and the invisible vampire in Maupassant's "The Horla." Concentrating on this mental image he succeeds in forming into a gaseous, invisible mass the monster of his imagination, but in so doing unwittingly creates a powerful artificial elemental with an insatiable lust for blood. Needless to say, the monster gets out of control and murder and mayhem ensue, bringing the story to a predictably violent conclusion.

Other outstanding vampire stories published by *Weird Tales* in the 1920s were Greye La Spina's suspenseful serial "Fettered" (run in four parts, commencing July 1926), Oscar Cook's fantastic yarn about a bloodsucking orchid-god, "Si Urag of the Tail" (July 1926), and Frank Owen's pseudo-Chinese folktale "The Tinkle of the Camel's Bell" (December 1928), in which an immortal woman has the power to drain the life out of everything she touches. Minor vampire stories from the same decade included Arlton Eadie's "The White Vampire" (September 1928), David H. Keller's "The Damsel and Her Cat" (April 1929), and Chester L. Saxby's "The Death Touch" (July 1929).

By the beginning of the 1930s, *Weird Tales* had firmly established itself as the premier source of new horror fiction, and had acquired a select band of regular contributors, including three who, because of their strong bias toward the vampire theme, I have dubbed The Vampire Masters. The first of this sanguinary trio to come under our scrutiny is Seabury Quinn, a prolific contributor to *Weird Tales* throughout its lifetime, and one whose stories consistently topped the readers' preference poll.

Quinn's first vampire story for the magazine was "The Man Who Cast No Shadow" (February 1927). Like the majority of this author's stories it featured the mercurial criminologist Jules de Grandin, who was one of the most popular characters ever to appear in the pages of "The Unique Magazine." As well as being the world's foremost phantom-fighter, the indomitable little Frenchman is a scientist and a physician; and his many other remarkable accomplishments often stand him in good stead during his weird exploits. Assisting him in his daring escapades is the stolid, Watson-like Dr. Trowbridge, who makes the perfect foil for his egotistical companion.

The duo's adversary in "The Man Who Cast No Shadow" is Count Czerny, a Transylvanian aristocrat on a life-or-death mission to the United States. The offspring of a noblewoman and her demon lover, he has remained perpetually in his prime for nearly a hundred years, but is doomed to die on the stroke of this century unless his vitality and youthful appearance are renewed by drinking the blood of a slaughtered virgin. Fortunately for his intended victim, his evil plans are thwarted by the vigilant detective, who had observed on their first meeting that the Count cast no reflection in a mirror and had a hairy palm—both tell-tale signs that he was a vampire.

Jules de Grandin's next brush with a vampire was in the poignant "Restless Souls" (October 1928). An unconventional love story, it concerns the cruel fate of a decent young woman who is raped and vampirized by a brutish man, and subsequently becomes one of the Undead. De Grandin learns the background to her tragic story when she falls in love with a young man suffering from a terminal heart condition, from whom she has been sucking small quantities of blood to keep her body whole and beautiful. Touched by the plight of the star-crossed lovers, the little Frenchman gives them his blessing for one last night of love, knowing that the youth is doomed anyway. The next morning the young man's demise is duly confirmed, and in a final act of compassion de Grandin dispatches the heartbroken vampiress, thereby releasing her from her unwanted life-in-death.

Another entertaining vampire story penned by Quinn in the 1920s was "The Silver Countess" (October 1929). Anthologized several times since, it owes much of its popularity to the author's inspired idea of a bloodsucking statue.

Quinn's quest for further unusual manifestations of the vampire continued into the thirties, beginning with "Satan's Stepson" (September 1931), a potpourri of classic horror motifs and effects which ran the whole gamut of emotions, from devine love to bestiality. Always one for giving his readers their money's worth, Quinn literally threw everything into this blockbuster of a yarn except the proverbial kitchen sink. The leading characters are a Satanic Russian spy and his reluctant bride, a lovely young woman called Sonia, who soon becomes the focus of the reader's sympathy. Indeed, no heroine since de Sade's Justine has suffered as much as she. First she is forced to marry this man whom she detests, is beaten and defiled by him on her wedding night, and worst of all is buried alive. Even when she is dug up and resuscitated through the timely intervention of Jules de Grandin, and marries her childhood sweetheart after her tormentor is seemingly killed, the nightmare is not yet over for the poor girl—for within a short while she is kidnapped by her former husband, who has mysteriously returned from the dead. Momentarily she is rescued, only to be abducted again and forced, by emotional blackmail, to offer herself as a sacrifice in a Black Mass ceremony, where, once again, her lovely body is defiled. There are even more twists and turns in the plot before de Grandin finally destroys this evil menace once and for all.

If the former was one of de Grandin's toughest cases, his next encounter with a member of the grisly guild of vampires was one of the most bizarre. The story was titled "Malay Horror," and it appeared in the September 1933 issue. For inspiration Quinn drew upon an ancient legend of the Far East, introducing his readers to a Malayan vampiress called a Penanggalan. According to legend this vicious female demon consists of just a woman's head with a length of esophagus hanging pendantly below the severed neck, from which depends a stomach sac. Of human origin, the Penanggalan retains an evil immortality by vampirizing the living, and has a wicked desire to make other women like itself. To achieve this aim the demon casts a spell over its chosen victim, whose neck then shows the marks of thongs upon it, leading to death by strangulation. The victim's head then parts company with her body at the point where the magic ligatures appeared on her neck, drawing as it does the esophagus and intestines behind it. The newly-created Penanggalan then flies off to join others of its kind.

Despite de Grandin's attempts to avert a similar fate befalling one of his clients—a young American woman—this unenviable lot is hers when she is pursued all the way to the United States by her demonic stepmother. However, the indefatigable phantom-fighter is not bested that easily; and when the demoness is eventually caught and destroyed, the heroine is restored to her former self by a miraculous operation, in which the amazing little Frenchman replaces her stomach and intestines in her carefully preserved body and stitches her head back on. And, believe it or not, this incredible piece of surgery is all done on a kitchen table by gaslight!

After a lean year for cases concerning vampires the August 1935 issue of *Weird Tales* saw the great detective back on the trail of his favorite occult adversary, in an adventure called "The Black Orchid." One of the most outré stories ever published in the magazine, it proved once again that Quinn's fertile imagination was unrivaled when it came to dreaming up original variations on the vampire theme. Providing the weird menace in this thrilling exploit is a vampirous orchid-plant, which, if placed on an open wound, blossoms into the likeness of a diminutive human figure, and then gorges itself on the blood of its debilitated victim.

Quinn's next incursion into vampire territory was with the sensational novelette "A Rival from the Grave" (January 1936), which effectively combined blood-chilling horror with sadistic eroticism. The central figure in this lurid melodrama is Elaine Taviton, a woman of almost inhuman sensuality whose whole existence is centered on her carnal appetites. While serving as a nurse during the First World War she seduces a submissive young man, and immediately sets the tone of their relationship by biting her lover on the wrist and sucking his blood, after which she bites her own wrist and commands him to drink some of *her* blood. After their marriage, life is one round of savage lovemaking, during which Elaine's bloodlust is insatiable. Five, ten, a dozen times a night she wounds her husband with her nails and drinks his blood. At other times she mutilates herself upon the hands and feet and under her left breast, and then lies with outstretched arms and folded feet while her husband, at her prompting, applies his lips to the wounds. "Love's crucifixion" she calls it!

Even after Elaine's sudden death there is no escape for the wretched man bound to her by blood. For when he remarries, Elaine's sex-seeking revenant comes between him and his bride in the nuptial bed, half strangling the woman who has taken her place and making savage love to her husband, proving that even death has not quenched her all-consuming lust. Elaine, however, is no longer the beautiful creature she was in life, but is hideously changed into a grotesque parody of womanhood. Belatedly called in on the case, de Grandin finds it no easy task to overcome the lustful revenant, and the climactic duel between the psychic sleuth and the villainess's psychoplasmic thought-form is one of the most thrilling sequences Quinn ever penned.

Two further adventures of Jules de Grandin from the late thirties also dealt with vampirism—"Pledged to the Dead" (October 1937) and "The Poltergeist of Swan Upping" (February 1939). Seabury Quinn also wrote several vampire stories in the 1940s, and these will be referred to in due course.

Now, on to our next Vampire Master—the incomparable Clark Ashton Smith. A poet of some distinction before turning to prose, he was a very different kind of writer to a conventional storyteller like Quinn. For Smith, style was paramount, and characterization and plot were of secondary importance. Though prolific—especially during the height of the Depression—he always eschewed crude hack work, and all his fiction bears the hallmark of craftsmanship. Contrary to the fashion of the day, he wrote most of his stories in ornate, gorgeously rich prose, in which the influence of Poe and the French Decadents was clearly evident. Though this might make Smith sound like the last person one would expect to find writing for the "despised" pulps—even a quality one like *Weird Tales*—he always had a faithful following among the regular readers. Admittedly, his poetic style was a little too sophisticated for many readers of the pulps, but for those fortunate enough to find the key to his imagination, a journey across the threshold was irresistible.

The first of C. A. Smith's stories to feature an exotic permutation of the vampire theme was "The End of the Story" (May 1930). Set in the imaginary French region of Averoigne, it describes how a young 18th-century law student succumbs to the charms of a beautiful lamia dwelling in the ancient vaults of a ruined chateau. Though there is hardly any plot, the witchery of Smith's prose holds the reader enthralled until the very last sentence. The same locale served as the setting for Smith's second vampire tale for the magazine, "A Rendezvous in Averoigne" (April-May 1931). A potent distillation of dreams and fantasy concerning an enchanted castle and its undead tenants, it has long been regarded as a classic.

After two vampire tales with the accent on fantasy rather than horror, Smith's third interpretation of the theme was a real spine-tingler, the unforgettable "The Vaults of Yoh-Vombis" (May 1932). Arguably this author's most gruesome story, it featured a horde of troglodyte vampires shaped like cushions, which drop onto the heads of a group of archeologists exploring ancient Martian catacombs and eat into their brains. Written in a more orthodox prose style than the one he usually employed, this story demonstrated Smith's incomparable ability to create and sustain a mood of lurking menace and unnamable horror. Like the insidious inspiration of an opium dream the horror creeps and grows, to spring at last upon the reader in all its totality.

For a later story, "Genius Loci" (June 1933), Smith chose a more commonplace setting; but this small concession to reality did not make the plot any less fantastic, as it was based on the alarming notion that some topographical locations display vampirish characteristics—in this instance an eerie meadow through which runs a sluggish stream ending abruptly in a stagnant pool flanked by weird-looking trees. Describing his fears about the sinister spot, the story's narrator remarks: "It has the air of a thirsty vampire, grown old and hideous with unutterable infamies." The longer he stays in the vicinity the more he becomes convinced that it is inhabited by a *genius loci*—an indwelling personality of a malign nature—which is waiting for the chance to drink him in. Less aware of the danger, his friends, a sensitive artist and his fiancée, yield to the meadow's lure, and their souls are absorbed.

In October 1933, *Weird Tales* published Smith's equally memorable short story "The Seed from the Sepulcher," which featured a blasphemous form of plant-life supposedly indigenous to the jungles of South America, and told of the dreadful fate which befalls an orchid-hunter who comes into contact with it. The doomed man's ordeal begins when the vampire-plant's spores germinate inside him and use his skull as a plant pot. Greedy roots spread all over his body and suck it dry of blood; and after a few days shoots begin to grow from the top of his head, branching out like antlers. The hideous metamorphosis is completed when a huge white blossom resembling the man's face appears among the topmost branches, and emits an hypnotic whining-sound. On this eerie note ends one of the most harrowing stories in the entire horror repertoire.

In a lighter vein is the same author's "The Flower-Women" (May 1935), a minor fantasy tale featuring exotic vampire-flowers with the semblance of beautiful, wanton women. Much stronger stuff, however, is "The Death of Ilalotha" (September 1937), which was the last vampire story Smith wrote for *Weird Tales* in the thirties. A unique blend of morbid eroticism and grotesque horror, it tells of a young man's midnight assignation with his dead lover, and of the grisly fate which befalls him when she metamorphoses into a ghoul-like lamia. Plot-wise, hardly anything happens until the climax, but the author's brilliant display of word-painting is a rare treat for all connoisseurs of decadent, erotic horror.

The third writer on whom I have bestowed the honorary title Vampire Master is C. L. Moore, who, as a complete unknown, was catapulted to fame with her very first story for *Weird Tales*, the sensational "Shambleau." The lead story in the November 1933 issue, it introduced this author's most famous character: Northwest Smith, outlaw of the spaceways. A tall, handsome man, his lithe, suntanned body scarred with the marks of countless battles, he is a born fighter, displaying in this and each of his subsequent adventures an amazing ability to win through against colossal odds. In the story's famous opening sequence, Northwest Smith rescues a frightened, scarlet-clad woman from a wild mob pursuing her through the narrow streets of an Earth colony on Mars. After using his blaster to disperse the crowd—on whose faces is a look of loathing and disgust—the space-adventurer takes the strange, turbaned fugitive to his quarters, little suspecting who—or *what*—he has befriended. Realization only comes after she removes her headdress to reveal a mass of writhing scarlet tendrils where her hair should be. With mixed feelings of rapture and revulsion, Smith is drawn into a passionate relationship with the Medusa-like vampiress, during which she gradually drains his life-force, bringing him almost to the point of death. But at the eleventh hour he is saved by his friend, Yarol, who destroys the evil Shambleau with a device similar to that used by the Greek hero to slay the Gorgon of mythology. Told in a colorful, dramatic fashion, it all adds up to one of the weirdest stories ever set down on paper.

After this sensational debut the readers of *Weird Tales* clamored for more stories about Northwest Smith; and the young authoress duly obliged, returning in the April 1934 issue with another adventure of extraordinary fascination and blood-chilling action titled "Black Thirst." Accosted by a Minga girl, one of a string of beautiful women bred up to the limit of loveliness and exported to the worlds of the galaxy, Northwest Smith is invited to the Minga stronghold to meet her master, the Alendar, the lone survivor of an ancient race akin to the vampire who has lived for countless ages breeding and devouring beauty. But Smith soon realizes he has walked into a trap, and when the Alendar attempts to absorb his identity as well, the space-outlaw's fate seems sealed. At the last moment, however, Smith's life is saved by the same Minga girl who had lured him into the vampire's clutches. With a self-sacrificial gesture she distracts the Alendar's concentration for the split second Smith needs to regain control of his senses, enabling him to destroy the assumed body of the Alendar with his ray-gun. This forces the evil consciousness of the vampire to withdraw to the dark dimension it originally came from.

One of the most interesting aspects of this particular story is the way beauty is depicted as a sinister force. There is one passage, for instance, which reads:

Beauty is as tangible as blood, in a way. It is a separate, distinct force that inhabits the bodies of men and women...a force so strong that it drives out all other forces and lives vampirishly at the expense of intelligence and goodness and conscience and all else.

As if to prove that her success was no flash in the pan, the brilliant newcomer penned another fantasy masterpiece for the magazine's May 1934 issue, the haunting "Scarlet Dream." Again it was a subtle, highly original variation on the vampire theme, with the same colorful imagery that had characterized her two previous stories. This time Northwest Smith found adventure, romance, and not a little horror in a frightening dreamworld entered via a dimensional door, the key to which was the strange pattern on a scarlet shawl. Not the least among the perils the intrepid space-adventurer had to contend with were cannibal trees and vampire grass.

So successful were Miss Moore's first few stories that in the October 1934 issue of *Weird Tales* the editor, Farnsworth Wright, was able to write this glowing tribute to his young protégée:

> Within one short year, C. L. Moore has become established as a giant among writers of weird fiction, taking rank with those who have heretofore been regarded as supreme: A. Blackwood, Arthur Machen, and H. P. Lovecraft; and today C. L. Moore is the favorite author of thousands of readers throughout the English speaking world.

Over the next five years Miss Moore secured her reputation with a string of masterly weird fantasies which have never been equalled in their emotional impact. Especially memorable is "Julhi" (March 1935), in which Apri, an insane girl, takes Northwest Smith through a dimensional gateway to meet her mistress, a glamorous Venusian vampiress, whose name gives the story its title. Apri, it transpires, is a human doorway whose mind can open the way for Julhi and her fellow vampires to enter our world and feed off the population; and only by strangling the unfortunate girl is Smith able to prevent this happening. Rather cleverly, the same plot was reworked in "The Cold Gray God" (October 1935), which concerns the attempted return of an exiled Martian god from his lair in another dimension. This time, however, the "key" used to open the gateway is a talisman.

By this time the more discerning readers of *Weird Tales* probably realized that this talented author was bent on exploring the tremendous potential of the vampire theme to the full, and was using the popular Northwest Smith stories to extend the frontiers of the theme to hitherto unsuspected horizons.

Further entires in the series continued this policy. In "Yvala" (February 1936), for instance, the vampire-haunted hero tangles with a modern Circe, who feeds on the humanity of all who come under her spell. In another adventure involving sorcery, "Lost Paradise" (July 1936), Northwest Smith helps a Selesian, a descendant of a race which once lived on the Moon, and in return is shown the Moon as it was in the days before a catastrophe left it dead and lifeless. Traveling back in time, he discovers that in the dim past the Earth's satellite was a pleasant, happy world with an atmosphere to support life, all of which had come about as a result of a bargain struck by the progenitors of the Moon-dwellers with a vampirish trinity of gods, who in return for their bounty demanded that after a short, contented cycle of life every man must go to the temple of the gods and, of his own free will, offer them his life. But when Smith's consciousness is transferred into the body of one of the young men about to make the sacrifice, he rebels against his fate and so breaks the contract, causing the angry gods to destroy the world their magical arts had created.

Northwest Smith's resilience was again sorely tested in "The Tree of Life" (October 1936). In this yarn the fearless space-outlaw is lured into an artificially-created circular world ruled over by a vampiric entity from another space-time continuum, who periodically comes to feed through a living incarnation of the fabled Tree of Life.

Jirel of Joiry, the swashbuckling heroine of Moore's other successful series for *Weird Tales,* also had a memorable encounter with a vampire in a story called "Hellsgarde" (April 1939). Always ready to cross swords with the powers of darkness, the fiery warrior-queen does battle with Alaric, who describes himself as "a hunter of Undeath." He and his kinsfolk lust after that dark force which the ghosts of the violent dead engender, and travel far and wide to quench their insatiable vampire-thirst.

Regrettably, this was C. L. Moore's last vampire story for "The Unique Magazine," as shortly afterwards she stopped writing weird fiction to concentrate on science fiction stories, many of which were written in collaboration with her husband, the late Henry Kuttner. Unquestionably, weird fiction's loss was science fiction's gain, but one cannot help wondering what weird masterpieces we might have had from this author's matchless imagination had things turned out differently. Nevertheless, in the few years Catherine Lucille Moore devoted to the weird fantasy tale she clearly demonstrated to those who were to follow in her footsteps that the scope of the vampire theme is virtually limitless.

Besides the magnificent Miss Moore, and the other two vampire specialists previously mentioned, many other well-known pulp-fiction authors contributed vampire stories to *Weird Tales* in the thirties. Generally speaking, the standard of writing in the magazine was much higher than in the previous decade, and some of the vampire stories dating from this period are now regarded as classics of their kind.

Robert E. Howard, one of the legendary figures of the pulp era, incorporated the vampire motif into a number of his action-packed stories, yet seldom used it as the main element. The nearest he got to writing a conventional vampire yarn was "The Horror from the Mound" in the May 1932 issue. A rather dull story by Howard's standards, it tells how the undead corpse of a Spanish nobleman is accidentally resurrected by a young American farmer digging for gold in an old Mexican burial mound. More typical of this author's rip-roaring style is the Solomon Kane adventure "The Hills of the Dead" (August 1930), in which the swashbuckling Puritan adventurer joins forces with an African witch-doctor to destroy a race of negroid vampires. In the story's spectacular climax the wily old fetish-man magically summons up thousands of vultures, which swoop down and tear the vampires to pieces.

Conan, the mighty barbarian hero of Howard's prototypal sword-and-sorcery stories, also had several near-fatal encounters with outlandish vampires of one sort or another. First of all, in "The Scarlet Citadel" (January 1933) he came up against a mind-sucking plant growing through the solid stone floor of a prison cell in a wizard's dungeon; then, in "The Hour of the Dragon" (which *Weird Tales* ran as a 5-part serial in 1935), he almost succumbed to a voluptuous vampiress, who, despite her glamorous appearance, was 10,000 years old; and, finally, in the 3-part serial "Red Nails" (July-October 1936) his pirate-girl companion, Valeria, was nearly killed by another deathless vampire-woman.

As in the previous decade, August Derleth continued to churn out a plethora of short stories for "The Unique Magazine" during the thirties. Those with a vampire motif included "Those Who Seek" (January 1932), "In the Left Wing" (June 1932), "Red Hands" (October 1932), "Nellie Foster" (June 1933), "The Drifting Snow" (February 1939), and "The Satin Mask" (January 1936). Only this last, in which a florentine mask vampirically drains the life from the person who wears it, shows any originality.

H. P. Lovecraft, the most respected author ever to appear in the hallowed pages of *Weird Tales*, rarely dipped into the pool of vampire lore in search of inspiration for his stylish horror tales, one of the few exceptions being "The Shunned House" (October 1937). Published posthumously, it concerns the history of a mysterious old house whose residents have for generations had their life-force sucked out of them by a huge, gelatinous vampire buried under the basement floor. Also, in his capacity of ghost-writer, Lovecraft shared much of the credit for Hazel Heald's gruesome addition to the Cthulhu Mythos, "The Horror in the Museum" (July 1933), in which a mad sculptor resurrects a vampire-god from centuries of slumber, and pays a grisly price for his folly. Another of Lovecraft's clients, Zealia B. Bishop, wrote—with a little help for her friend—the equally sensational "Medusa's Coil" (January 1939). Overwritten and wildly melodramatic, it features a vampirish femme fatale called Marceline, whose serpent-like hair has a life of its own.

Lovecraft (through the agency of a dream) also provided the inspiration for Frank B. Long's major work in the 1930s, "The Horror from the Hills," which *Weird Tales* ran in two parts, commencing January 1931. With a plot that staggers the imagination, this vintage classic chronicles the incredible history of Chaugnar Faugn, a powerful vampire-god from the fourth dimension. Having originally manifested on our planet at the dawn of time, this ghoulish entity has found a modern incarnation in a grotesque stone idol, which comes to life after it is transported to a museum in the United States. After an orgy of blood-drinking its power increases at an alarming rate, making it a threat to the safety of the whole world. Although great demands are made on the reader's ability to suspend disbelief, the spectacular way in which this menace is finally combated makes an exciting conclusion to a story full of thought-compelling complexities and awesome speculation.

An earlier vampire yarn by Long, "The Ocean Leech," was chosen as the "Weird Story Reprint" for the June 1937 issue. Thematically similar to the horror stories of William Hope Hodgson, it features a fearsome octopoidal sea creature which comes aboard a ship and decimates the crew. The monster's vampire-like nature is stressed by the fascinated repulsion the victims feel in its presence, and their sense of ecstasy when being drained of their life-blood.

Lovecraft's foremost disciple in the mid-thirties was Robert Bloch, who was then just starting out on a highly successful literary career. One of his earliest Cthulhu Mythos stories for *Weird Tales* was "The Shambler from the Stars" (September 1935), in which a hapless Providence scholar (a joke reference to Lovecraft) has his blood drained by a vampirous "thing." Another Lovecraft pastiche by Bloch, "The Mannikin" (April 1937), also has strong vampiric implications.

Science fiction pioneer Edmond Hamilton, a stalwart of *Weird Tales* for most of its lifetime, had a penchant for extraterrestrial vampires of immense size and power. For example, in "The Earth-Owners" (August 1931), super-intelligent cloud-like beings fight for the ownership of our world. Like huge, black vampires they hang menacingly over the Earth's cities, and suck out the life-force of the inhabitants. Providentially, their plan to denude Earth of all life is thwarted when huge globes of light, the benign "Earth-Owners," come to the rescue. On an even larger scale is the vampire-like force in the same author's "The Comet–Drivers" (February 1930). Here the menace to human life is a giant comet from the void of space, which, like a cosmic vampire, speeds through space looting the lives of universe after universe.

When Hamilton wanted a change of pace from his frenetic interplanetary yarns he wrote straight weird fiction under the pseudonym of Hugh Davidson. Using this byline he penned a short story called "Vampire Village" (November 1932) and a 4-part serial titled "The Vampire Master," which commenced in the October 1933 issue.

Even more prolific than Hamilton—some say that his output even surpassed that of Edgar Wallace—was the old-time pulpster Harold Ward. Of his fifteen stories for *Weird Tales* the best-remembered is "The House of the Living Dead" (March 1932). A no-holds-barred mixture of violent action and supernatural terror, with a dash of sex thrown in for good measure, it features a master-occultist called Doctor Lessman and his soul-mate, the lovely Meta. Both, it transpires, are ancient Egyptians whose souls have survived down the ages by a combination of metempsychosis and vampirism.

A more conventional manifestation of the vampire is to be found in the same author's "The Life-Eater" (June 1937). At one point in the story the hero awakens to find that—

Upon his breast rested a *thing*—a horrible, nauseous, formless monstrosity, shapeless, faceless, headless. Yet it had a face and head, for its eyes were the eyes that were glaring into his own. And, too, it had a mouth—a red gash framed by leathery lips. It was pressed against his own in a clammy, vacuum-like kiss. It was lapping his breath, sucking the vitality from his body, deflating it until it was rapidly growing as flat as a bursted tire. Its long, sinuous arms were fastened about him, its legs wrapped, leech-like, about his own.

Deathless prose it may not have been, but the majority of readers lapped it up.

Another regular contributor to *Weird Tales* in the 1930s was Kirk Mashburn. Discovered, like so many others, through Farnsworth Wright's farsighted policy of seeking out and promoting new talent, he is chiefly remembered today for one story alone, "Placide's Wife" (November 1931), in which the twin themes of vampirism and werewolfism were rather ambiguously combined. The favorable response to the story led to a sequel, "The Last of Placide's Wife" (September 1932), in which the undead spouse was finally laid to rest. Two other stories by this author which contained a vampire element were "The Vengeance of Ixmal" (March 1932) and "De Brignac's Lady" (February 1933). The latter was captioned "A story of baby vampires: infant marauders belonging to the Undead!" It was just as ludicrous as it sounds, and Mashburn's career swiftly took a nose-dive.

A more talented addition to *Weird Tales*' stable of writers in the thirties was Henry Kuttner, who made his debut with that classic of gnawing horror, "The Graveyard Rats." His subsequent sales to the magazine included two vampire stories, "The Secret of Kralitz" (October 1936) and "I, the Vampire" (February 1937), both of which had an unusual approach to the theme.

In the late thirties, with Robert E. Howard and Lovecraft both dead, *Weird Tales* was in desperate need of someone to fill their shoes. One newcomer who briefly looked like he might make the grade was Thorp McClusky, whose very first contribution to the magazine was a fast-paced serial titled "Loot of the Vampire" (June-July 1936). Though somewhat naive by today's standards, it was well received at the time, prompting one enthusiastic reader to make the comment that is was "like *Dracula* with the boring bits cut out!" However, McClusky's greatest success came with his next story, "The Crawling Horror" (November 1936), which featured a vampiric monster called a Vombis. Like an amorphous mass of slime in appearance, this repulsive-looking entity dissolves its victims into a consistency similar to its own, prior to absorbing them body and soul. It also possesses the ability to assume the form of the person it has just absorbed—a cunning deception which assists it greatly in its quest for further victims.

Amelia Reynolds Long, one of *Weird Tales*' small band of women writers, had several vampire tales to her credit in the 1930s. The most unusual was "The Thought-Monster" (March 1930), in which an artificial elemental waxed strong by absorbing human thoughts. Less imaginatively conceived were "The Undead" (August 1931) and "Flapping Wings of Death" (June 1935).

One story guaranteed to make even the most phlegmatic reader squirm in his seat is Mearle Prout's "The House of the Worm," from the October 1933 issue. Definitely not for the squeamish, it concerns a hideous blight of nocturnally-active maggots which are menacing a remote rural district. Embodied in this nauseous symbol of death and corruption is a vicious thought-vampire which has been created by the collective imaginations of a group of religious fanatics, from whose control it has escaped. Caught in the path of this advancing tide of death, a whole forest and the surrounding hamlets—including the human inhabitants—are sucked dry of life, until they are reduced to a mass of maggot-ridden putrefaction. In the end this creeping menace is halted and destroyed by fire.

Dorothy Quick, an intermittent contributor of short stories and poems to *Weird Tales* throughout the thirties, was at her most diabolical in "Strange Orchids" (March 1937). A macabre extension of the carnivorous plant theme, it describes how an evil madman implants an orchid-plant into the stomach of a beautiful woman, with the result that it absorbs her color, her brain, even her soul. And when it has exhausted all she has to give—it blooms!

Hereditary vampirism is the theme of "The Brotherhood of Blood" (May 1932) by the versatile pulpeteer Hugh B. Cave. On her twenty-eighth birthday an attractive young woman is visited by the vampire form of her dead mother, and is afflicted with the family curse of vampirism, which she, in turn, must pass on to her nearest and dearest. In a denouement full of pathos the reluctant vampiress is forced to suck the blood of the man she loves, and dies tragically after being lured into a trap set by rejected suitor.

One of the finest vampire stories "The Unique Magazine" ever published is Carl Jacobi's "Revelations in Black" (April 1933). Well-crafted—almost Victorian in style–it is notable for an updating of the old superstition that a vampire's image is not reflected in a mirror. Instead, it is a photographic plate which exposes the vampire's identity.

Arthur J. Burks, who wrote many lurid horror stories for the pulps, was renowned for his unusual plots; and his offbeat vampire yarn "The Room of Shadows" in the May 1936 issue of *Weird Tales* was no exception. The villain of the piece is Lun Yurka, an incredibly-old Eurasian vampire domiciled in the United States. Ostensibly the head of a call-girl racket, he vampirizes all the women who fall into his clutches and mysteriously changes them into Chinese sleeve-dogs. Thereafter, anyone bitten by these diminutive vampires is similarly transformed, and joins the master-vampire's army of canine familiars. The twist ending, where the person narrating the story has his body appropriated by the cunning Lun Yurka, is just one of many surprises in this unique thriller.

For a time in the thirties *Weird Tales* supplemented its diet of horror stories with a fascinating selection of weird-scientific yarns—and none were weirder than Donald Wandrei's "The Fire Vampires" (February 1933). In the year 2321, Earth is attacked by a dictatorial visitor from another solar system, who issues a message that he intends to claim the lives of thousands of Earth's inhabitants as tribute. Subsequently, all over the world, people are struck down by balls of fire and immolated. The perpetrators of this fiery onslaught are vicious electrical beings constituted of pure energy, who feed on human life-force. Brought to its knees by this savage attack, the world seems doomed to become a slave-planet of the alien dictator and his fire vampires, until an American scientist comes up with a desperate plan to defeat them.

Pseudo-science and horror are also brilliantly combined in P. Schuyler Miller's "Spawn" (August 1939). Based on the Fortean theory that pure life travels from planet to planet in spores, it tells what happens when three spores fall on Earth. The first lands on a mountain range and creates a huge stone-monster; the second lands in the ocean, bringing to life a terrifying sea-monster; and the third falls on the body of the dead dictator, Nicholas Svadin, as he lies in state. Great havoc and loss of life are caused by the first two, but ultimately the greatest threat to humanity comes from the resurrected despot, who is transformed into a vampire with the power to bud off duplicates of himself. In the story's sensational climax, revolutionaries opposed to Svadin break into his palace and, catching him without any clothes on, see him as he really is:

He was corpse-white, blotched with the purple-yellow of decay, bloated with the gases of death. Svadin—undead—unhuman—and around his feet ten gibbering simulacra of himself—ten pulpy, fish-white monsters of his flesh, their slit-mouths red with blood.

More subtle in its weirdness is Leslie F. Stone's forgotten gem "When the Flame-Flowers Blossomed" (November 1935), a highly original story told from the viewpoint of intelligent plant vampires. Another remarkable effort by a comparatively minor author was A. W. Calder's "Song of

Death" (June 1938), an eerie story about an alluring vampire-song which proves fatal to all who perform it on the radio. Responsibility for the mysterious deaths is eventually attributed to soul-sucking musical vibrations from another dimension, which have been attracted to our planet by powerful radio transmissions.

Other vampire tales published in *Weird Tales* in the 1930s included "River of Lost Souls" (May 1930) by Robert C. Sandison; "The Vrykolakas" (April 1932) by Robert C. Sandison; "Ghouls of the Sea" (March 1934) by J. B. S. Fullilove; "The Nightmare Road" (March 1934) by Florence Crow; "Return to Death" (January 1936) by J. Wesley Rosenquest; "The Sealed Casket" (March 1935) by Richard F. Searight; "The Spider's Web" (June 1935) by John Scott Douglas; "In a Graveyard" (October 1935) by E. & O. Binder; "The Amulet of Hell" (October 1935) by Robert Leonard Russell; "The Horror Undying" (May 1936) by Manly Wade Wellman; "Isle of the Undead" (October 1936) by Lloyd Arthur Eshbach; "The Doom of the House of Duryea" (October 1936) by Earl Peirce, Jr.; "Brother Lucifer" (November 1936) by Chandler H. Whipple; "The Woman in Room 607" (January 1937) by Thorp McClusky; "School for the Unspeakable" (September 1937) by Manly Wade Wellman; "The Silver Coffin" (January 1939) by Robert Barbour Johnson; "Cross of Fire" (May 1939) by Lester del Rey; "The Hollow Moon" (May 1939) by Everil Worrell; and "Spanish Vampire" (September 1939) by E. Hoffman Price.

A major rival of *Weird Tales* in the early thirties was Clayton Publishing Corporation's *Strange Tales*, edited by Harry Bates. The first issue, launched in September 1931, was packed with top quality stories by popular authors. Understandably, with competition so keen on the newsstands, there had been no time for *Strange Tales* to slowly build up a coterie of specialist writers as *Weird Tales* had done in the 1920s, so it simply lured them away from its prestigious rival by offering higher fees—a policy which ensured it got all the best stories these authors produced. Had the magazine survived longer it may well have supplanted *Weird Tales* as America's premier weird fiction magazine. As it was, the sudden collapse of the Clayton publishing empire caused it to fold after only seven issues.

Of the fifty-five stories *Strange Tales* managed to cram into its short run, at least ten contained a vampire element. Among them was a refreshingly different treatment of the theme, Victor Rousseau's "A Cry from Beyond" (September 1931), in which a malicious astral shell sucks the blood of a sleeping child by animating her doll.

The most sensational vampire story to originate from this magazine was undoubtedly Hugh B. Cave's "Murgunstrumm" (January 1933). Murgunstrumm is the name of the gargoyle-like landlord of an old, decayed country tavern called The Gray Toad Inn, which is the hideout for a family of vampire brothers who prey on rich young society women. After a night on the town the immaculately-dressed vampires lure the hypnotized girls back to the Inn to ravish them and drink their blood. Afterwards, the victims' lifeless bodies are handed over to the subhuman landlord, who takes them to the cellar and feasts upon them like a ghoul.

Only slightly less gruesome is the same author's "Stragella" in the June 1932 issue. In contrast to the aforementioned story, the action takes place on board a tramp steamer, the crew of which have all succumbed to the deadly attentions of a trio of vampires—an old man, a hag-like woman, and a sensuous gypsy girl called Stragella.

Another old-time pulpster with a genuine flair for creating images of sheer terror was Paul Ernst. Amazingly prolific, he wrote scores of stories throughout the thirties; but it is doubtful if any surpassed his novelette "The Duel of the Sorcerers" (*Strange Tales*, March 1932). Replete with mystery and horror, it chronicled the weird crimes of a college professor's evil assistant, who has learnt how to circumvent death and make himself into a vampire after finding the lost chapter of a rare occult treatise by Cagliostro. As with most of Ernst's fiction this story's success owes much to the author's fine story sense and his inspired talent to evoke an emotional mood and atmosphere.

C. A. Smith's major contribution to *Strange Tales* was an ultra-weird vampire tale, "The Hunters from Beyond." Published in the October 1932 issue, it featured those vicious denizens of the astral plane, elementals, about whom Smith had this to say: "They quest for men's souls—their brains too—it is their nourishment: they are creatures who prey on the minds of the insane or weak." At the end of the story all this—and more—is confirmed when a young artists' model falls into their clutches, and is drained of all life, thought, emotion and memory, until she is like an empty shell.

In Francis Flagg's erotic horror story "The Smell" (*Strange Tales*, January 1932) a man is intoxicated by an unspeakably foul yet, at the same time, desirable and piercingly sweet odor that fills his bedroom each night. Unable to sleep, he lays on his bed and luxuriates in the smell; but when morning comes he feels sick and devitalized. Later, the source of the smell, a succubus, is sensed by touch and hearing, yet remains invisible. Thenceforward the nocturnal visitations take on a sexual aspect; and while the man caresses the demon's long, sinuous body it whispers things in his ear that drive him into an ecstasy of madness. At length he loses all resistance to the sex-vampire, and dies of fright when it becomes visible.

Two other entertaining vampire yarns that originally came from this short-lived magazine were Marion Brandon's "The Dark Castle" (September 1931) and Philip Hazleton's "After Sunset" (November 1931). The latter broke new ground by telling the story from the viewpoint of the vampire, allegedly the first pulp story to do so.

Another relatively short-lived pulp magazine of the inter-war years, *Ghost Stories* (1926-32), occasionally seasoned its bland diet of fictional and "true" ghost stories with vampire tales, of which the following are a representative selection: "The Vampire of Oakdale Ridge" (December 1926) by Robert W. Sneddon: "The Mark on the Seaman's Throat" (March 1929) by The Rev. Arthur Ford: "The Sign on the Throat" (a 3-part serial commencing October 1929) by Jennings Holt; and "Park Avenue Vampire" (a 4-part serial commencing July 1930) by Ramon Dawson.

The science fiction pulps of the 1920s and '30s also found a place for occasional pieces of weird fiction, which were labelled "different" stories to distinguish them from the usual fare associated with these publications. Among these "interlopers" were several quality vampire stories, including two by the ubiquitous C. A. Smith—"Marooned on Andromeda" and "The Demon of the Flower." The former, from *Wonder Stories*, October 1930, is a colorful piece of descriptive prose concerning the amazing forms of quasi-vampiric plant life found on the planet Andromeda; while the latter, from *Astounding Stories*, December 1933, is about an omnipotent plant-deity that feeds exclusively on human blood.

Other notable vampire tales that appeared in sf/fantasy magazines during this era were A. Hyatt Verrill's "Vampires of the Desert" (*Amazing Stories*, December 1929), Franklin W. Ryan's "The Last Earl" (*Amazing Stories*, January 1933), and Robert E. Howard's "The Garden of Fear" (*Marvel Tales*, July-August 1934). In this last the barbarian hero encounters the lone survivor of a race of vampires, who has made his abode in a stone tower surrounded by a field of blood-drinking flowers.

Sex and Sadism

With the rare exception of quality publications like *Weird Tales* and *Strange Tales*, the majority of American horror/mystery magazines published during the decade prior to the Second World War were cheap and nasty, catering for the least intellectual section of the reading market. Known collectively as the weird menace pulps, they were vehicles for highly sensational stories of torture, flagellation, and voyeuristic sex.

The leading purveyors of this type of fiction were *Terror Tales* and its sister magazine *Horror Stories*, both founded by Popular Publications in the mid-thirties. Virtually all the stories that appeared in these two periodicals were written to a carbon-copy formula, with little variation in the plots. Obviously, such a monotonous diet—no matter how titillating the presentation—would not have appealed to the connoisseur of the horror story; but for the newly-literate masses, who formed the vast majority of the magazines' readers, it was just the right fare to help them forget the real horror of the Depression. Indeed, one reader more articulate than the rest spoke for them all when he wrote in to say: "It is my belief that most readers react more strongly to suggestions of physical torture and conceptions of monstrous grotesque beings than they do to the supernatural and all the vague business of death." The editors seemed to agree, as the supernatural had no place in the majority of stories, and a theme like vampirism was exploited mainly for its sexual overtones.

The following excerpt from Nat Schachner's "Thirst of the Ancients" (*Terror Tales*, February 1935) is typical of the way vampirism was depicted:

She was coming to drink the last remnants of my blood! I heard the faint rustle of the woman as she thrust her head closer to mine. A muscle twitched in my bare neck. My head was rigid, my eyes were closed. A burning iron entered my throat, just above the jugular. A tooth! Warm stickiness flowed out, was draining... In spite of steeled will, I jerked uncontrollably. The cold bare arms tightened on my body. Sharp teeth nuzzled hungrily deeper, closer to the jugular. I felt the greedy crunch of bone through cartilage. My blood spurted. I felt faint, sick with irrepressible horror.

Terror Tales published several vampire stories in a similar vein, including Arthur Leo Zagat's "Thirst of the Living Dead" (November 1934) and Raymond Whetstone's "The Thirsty Dead" (March 1935). *Horror Stories* kept pace with John H. Knox's "Men Without Blood" (January 1935), Ralston Shields' "Daughter of the Devil" (October-

November 1937), Cornell Woolrich's "Vampire's Honeymoon" (August-September 1939), Wayne Rogers' "Dracula's Bride" (February 1941), and a gruesome yarn by Wyatt Blassingame called "Goddess of Crawling Horrors" (February-March 1937), which featured a beautiful yet deadly vampiress, on the back of whose hand rested a great hideous worm— its head buried in her flesh.

Dime Mystery Stories, another leading vehicle for sadistic horror tales, ran the following sex-oriented vampire stories: "They Drink Blood" (August 1934) by Norvell Page, "Vampires Can't Die!" (February 1935) by E. G. Morris, and "Little Miss Dracula" (August 1938) by Ralston Shields. This last concerned the ironic fate of Count Nigel Becker-Hazi, who kept his rich, sensuous wife contented with simulated vampire-lovemaking, only to succumb, in the end, to the fatal charms of a seductress who really was a vampire.

To round off this cursory glance at the weird menace pulps, here is a further selection of vampire-story titles—this time from cheap imitations of the "Big Three": "Vampire Meat" by Fred C. Painton (*Doctor Death*, April 1935); "Death Reign of the Vampire-King" by Grant Stockbridge (*Spider Magazine*, November 1935); "Coyote Woman" by Charles Warren (*Ace Mystery*, July 1936); "Prey of the Nightborn" by Justin Case (*Spicy Mystery Stories*, September 1936); "Vampire Bite" by Greye La Spina (*Bull's-Eye Detective*, Spring 1939); and "Purr of the Cat" by Justin Case (*Spicy Mystery Stories*, March 1942). Justin Case, incidentally, was a pseudonym used by Hugh B. Cave.

Not-So-Weird Tales

The vampire stories of those writers whose work was considered good enough for book publication in the 1930s were, almost without exception, of inferior quality to the best that the pulpsters produced. Some may have been superior as literature—though even this is debatable—but most of them lacked the invention, the daring plots, and the eerie thrills of their down-market counterparts.

The best-known British vampire stories from the thirties are Sydney Horler's "The Believer" (1931), Lady Eleanor Smith's "Satan's Circus" (1932), and Robert Thurston Hopkins' "The Vampire of Woolpit Grange" (1938). Obscurer stories include Lewis Spence's "The Red Flasket" (1932), D. H. Lawrence's "The Lovely Lady" (1932), Walter Starkie's "The Old Man's Story" (1933), Christopher Blayre's "Zum Wildbad" (1934), Flora Mayor's "Fifteen Charlotte Street" (1935), Frederick Cowles' "The Horror of Abbot's Grange" (1936) and "The

Vampire of Kaldenstein" (1938), and E. R. Punshon's "The Living Stone" (1939).

Some of these stories—especially those in the latter group—are quite interesting. Spence's overlooked piece (tucked away in his collection *The Archer in the Arras and Other Tales of Mystery*) is about an old man whose vitality is restored by drinking the blood of virgins; Blayre's story (from an even more obscure collection, *Some Women at the University*) hints at lesbianism; Mayor's tale (from her collection *The Room Opposite and Other Tales of Mystery & Imagination*) is about a doctor who physically drains his patients' energy after subduing them by hypnotism; Hopkins' yarn (which originally appeared in an obscure magazine called *Fireside Ghost Stories*) features a vampiric portrait; and Punshon's piece (from the April 1939 issue of *The Cornhill Magazine*) is about a block of stone formerly used for blood sacrifices, which periodically comes to life and devours any people or animals that approach it.

A further handful of British vampire stories can be found scattered about the "Creeps" series of anthologies, which Philip Allan published in the mid-thirties. The eighth volume in the series, *Monsters* (1934), contains "Two Old Women" by Vivian Meik, which combines vampirism with black magic; the eleventh volume, *Thrills* (1935), includes "Dr. Horder's Room" by Patrick Carleton, in which the ghost of a 16th-century cabalist attacks young men in their sleep and vampirically drains their life essence; and the twelfth volume, *Tales of Fear* (1935), boasts three stories with a vampire element: "The Thing from the Pit" by Arthur Stafford Aylmer, "The Horror in the Pond" by A. D. Avison, and "The Silent Inn" by Geoffrey Wyndham Lewis. The first two feature blood-drinking monsters; the third is about a strange inn run by vampires.

Nearly all the vampire novels published in Britain and the United States during this decade were blatantly contrived potboilers revolving around stock situations. Typical examples are Gaston Leroux's *The Kiss That Killed* (1934), Sydney Horler's *The Vampire* (1935), A. Hyder's *Vampires Overhead* (1935), Ridgwell Cullum's *The Vampire of N'Gobi* (1936), Norah Burke's *The Scarlet Vampire* (1936), J. U. Nicholson's *Fingers of Fear* (1937), and R. R. Ryan's *The Echo of a Curse* (1939). Nicholson's lurid shocker, about an upper crust English family cursed with an uncontrollable bloodlust, is overwritten to such a degree that one suspects the author might have intended it as a parody of the genre.

Far superior than any of the aforementioned is A. Merritt's *Creep, Shadow*, which had its first book publication in 1934. Although not primarily concerned with vampirism, this gripping novel does contain a memorable sequence in which vampirism plays a key part. After a string of nightmarish experiences on the astral plane, the hero's shadowy astral form, acting under the control of a modern-day sorceress, is sent back to the earth-plane to vampirize the woman he loves. "Creep, Shadow! Thirst, Shadow!, Hunger, Shadow!", the witch-woman exhorts him; but the purity of his fiancée's love is stronger than the magic of the sorceress, and the spell is broken before any harm is done.

On similar lines is Jack Mann's weird thriller *Maker of Shadows* (1938). For centuries, an evil Druid living in a remote Scottish village has secured immortality for himself by absorbing the life essence of human sacrifices to the ancient gods he worships. The souls of his victims subsequently haunt the neighborhood in the form of shadows.

A Dying Tradition?

After the peak years of the thirties the popularity of the American weird-fantasy pulps declined dramatically in the 1940s. One by one, established magazines ceased publication, their untimely demise hastened by the wartime paper shortage. Against the odds, *Weird Tales* survived, despite the loss of its guiding light, Farnsworth Wright, who died in 1940. His successor as editor, Dorothy McIlwraith, temporarily put the magazine on a sounder financial footing, but could do nothing to halt the steady deterioration in the quality of the stories.

In this decade, as in the previous one, the major contributor to the magazine was the veteran pulpster Seabury Quinn. Writing better than ever, his great imaginative power disciplined by a sense of balance in composition, he produced some exceptional stories, several of which had a vampire motif.

In "Mortmain" (January 1940) he introduced his readers to a Mongolian vampire called a ch'ing shih. Almost indestructible, vampires of this species are either the souls or corpses of black magicians, or (as in this case) the victims of sorcerous spells. For long periods they seem to be dead, but revive periodically to nourish themselves on blood. Even if decapitated or staked these resilient vampires can still materialize as long as any part of them remains intact, which leaves incineration as the only means to destroy them.

Quinn's "Vampire Kith and Kin" (May 1949) is also well-crafted, but his outstanding vampire story from the forties is undoubtedly "Clair de Lune" (November 1947), which still stands as the definitive portrait of a female psychic sponge. Apart from the ubiquitous Jules de Grandin, the story's main character is a celebrated actress, renowned for her great—and seemingly ageless—beauty. When de Grandin meets her at a social function he recognizes her as a notorious femme fatale whom he had met many years ago, yet she has not aged one bit. He recalls that she was involved in a scandal concerning the death of her masseuse, a strong, healthy young woman, who had been hired by the actress after she had been smitten with a strange wasting disease that caused her to age rapidly. But in two weeks the masseuse was dead and her employer had been miraculously restored to her former youth and beauty. De Grandin's suspicions that the same sinister events are about to repeat themselves are confirmed when he examines a teenage girl, who since her association with the actress has become a physical wreck. After questioning the girl, the little Frenchman learns that she has developed a crush on the actress and visits her regularly. On these occasions the fatal beauty appears very fatigued, and lies languorously on a chaise-longue, attired only in a flimsy negligee. Completely under the spell of the older woman, the infatuated teenager reads to her while they lovingly hold hands; and after tea they take a nap together, cradled in each other's arms. It is then that the transference of vitality takes place, leaving the victim in a state of collapse and investing the vampiress with renewed vigor. But through de Grandin's timely intervention the girl is saved from her inevitable fate, and the vampiress, deprived of her supply of energy, rapidly ages into an old hag.

Clark Ashton Smith, another writer inseparably linked with *Weird Tales*, was little heard of in the forties, but his engaging fantasy "The Enchantress of Sylaire," in the July 1941 issue, showed that he had not lost his old touch. A youth who has ventured into a magic realm ruled over by an enchantress named Sephora is accosted on his way to her castle by a shape-shifting sorcerer, who proceeds to warn him that Sephora is an unthinkably-old and hideous lamia who has created for herself a glamorous appearance in order to seduce young men and feed on their vital forces. However, the youth suspects that the sorcerer is trying to keep her to himself, and when he eventually meets the stunning enchantress decides: better one night of love with her than a thousand nights of tedium and futility in the outside world.

The action in Thorp McClusky's "The Graveyard Horror" (March 1941) is centered around a cemetery, in which are buried the bodies of two vampires—one male, the other female. At night they leave their graves in spirit form, gaining egress through two small holes in the grave mound. Two men who had known the undead couple in their former existence succeed in dispatching the male vampire, but the vampiress proves harder to pin down. In the dead of night they dig up her coffin and stake the body inside, but the evil spirit—the animating force—has previously quit the shell, and unseen in the night laughs with triumph at their futile efforts. However, the last laugh is with the vampire-hunters, for they know that the spirit must return to the body before dawn. Horrified yet fascinated, they watch as a gray mist enters the corpse through the nostrils, and life slowly returns to the cadaver. At the same time the stake is forced out and the wound vanishes. Stung into action, one of the men grasps the stake and hammers it back in, until it grinds against the solid wood of the casket. This time the job is done properly, and the vampiress is finally laid to rest. One further particular worth mentioning is that nowhere throughout the narrative does the author use the word "vampire," which is some feat considering the content of the story.

Robert Bloch, who had by the 1940s forsaken his Lovecraft pastiches in favor of slick stories in a style all his own, contributed two fine stories to *Weird Tales* in this decade, "The Bat is My Brother" (November 1944) and "The Bogey Man Will Get You" (March 1946). The former, which is exceedingly well-crafted, opens dramatically with the narrator, Graham Keene, describing his horror at finding himself inside a coffin, buried alive! Then follows a graphic description of his frantic bid to escape from this premature incarceration, which meets with success due to the shallowness of the grave. But this is only the beginning of Keene's ordeal, for he meets a pale stranger in the cemetery who coolly informs him: "I am a vampire...and so are you!" Stunned and half disbelieving, he allows the unknown man to take him back to his abode, where he learns the full story. The stranger, it transpires, is a centuries-old vampire who plans to create an army of the Undead, with the ultimate aim of world domination; and he has chosen Keene, who he had earlier vampirized, to assist him in the army's recruitment. Revolted by the stranger's chilling discourse, Keene hatches a plan to get his revenge; and, pretending to be won over to the vampire's ideas, lures him to a graveyard on the pretext that he has found a likely recruit to their new order. The two of them dig up a coffin which, according to Keene, contains the body of a man who has just been buried; but when it is opened there is nothing inside. Then, in a flash, Keene strikes. He coshes the vampire and shoves him into the empty coffin, seals it up, and buries it under six feet of wet earth. Thus he is fittingly avenged, for the vampire cannot die from suffocation as a normal person would, but, undying, must suffer horribly as his body slowly decays. At length, after months of ceaseless torment— made more unbearable by pangs of red hunger—comes the added horror of charnel worms pouring through the cracks in the decayed casket to feast on the still-living flesh.

A similar scenario forms the basis for E. Everett Evans' "The Undead Die" (July 1948), which, like Bloch's story, involves a victim taking revenge on the fiend who had vampirized him. After exploring the cellars of a ruined castle, a young couple, Robert and Lisa, are overpowered and vampirized by an undead nobleman, and thereafter are forced to live the lives of vampires—bond-slaves of The Master. But their undying love for each other, the one pure thing left in their lives, brings solace into an otherwise hateful existence, earning them the pity of the mighty Earth Elemental, who aids Robert in breaking The Master's hold over them. Even so, there is no escape from their undead state; and they continue to live as vampires for centuries, until the accidental death of Lisa and the broken-hearted Robert's suicide (by staking himself) brings their tragic story to a close. One suspects that even hardened horror fans would find themselves with a lump in their throats after reading such a poignant little tale.

A fascinating novelette that aroused considerable interest when it appeared in the July 1942 issue was Manly Wade Wellman's "Coven." Set during the American Civil War, it is based on Mountain White legends concerning a winged, horned entity which allegedly organized men and women into black-magic covens. More germane to the vampire theme is an episode preceding the main narrative in which a young Confederate soldier helps two Yankee vampire-hunters locate and dispatch a female vampire.

Vampirism also plays a small but significant part in H. P. Lovecraft's short novel *The Case of Charles Dexter Ward*, which *Weird Tales* ran in two installments, commencing May 1941. Mainly revolving around magical experiments to raise the long-dead from their "essential salts," a vampire element is introduced into the plot when the hero's ancestor, a notorious 18th-century sorcerer, is revivified, and for a while has to drink human blood to build up his strength.

The only other outstanding vampire tale published by "The Unique Magazine" in the forties was Henry Kuttner's macabre satire "Masquerade" (May 1942), which was later successfully adapted for television. Less effective stories by other *Weird Tales'* regulars were "Return of the Undead" (July 1943) by Otis Adelbert Kline and Frank B. Long, "Interim" (July 1947) by Ray Bradbury, "The Occupant of the Crypt" (September 1947) by August Derleth and Mark Schorer, and "The Antimacassar" (May 1949) by Greye La Spina.

The only fantasy-oriented pulp magazine to seriously challenge *Weird Tales'* supremacy during this period was *Unknown* (later called *Unknown Worlds*). More literary than its legendary rival, it broke new ground by publishing slick stories satirizing standard weird-fantasy themes. Typical of the fare that was offered is Robert Bloch's "The Cloak" (May 1939), a black comedy about a man who goes to a fancy dress ball wearing an authentic vampire's cape, which induces in him a desire to drink blood. The twist ending—where a real vampire turns the tables on him—is expertly concealed until the last moment.

Another characteristic vampire story from this magazine is Manly Wade Wellman's "When it was Moonlight" (February 1940). Not to be taken too seriously, it tells of an imaginary encounter between Edgar Allan Poe and a female vampire who is afraid of the dark. An equally unlikely confrontation occurs in the same author's "The Devil is Not Mocked" (*Unknown Worlds*, June 1943), in which Count Dracula vanquishes a troop of Nazi soldiers.

Not all the stories in *Unknown* were humorous, however. Occasionally the editor slipped in a really harrowing piece, such as P. Schuyler Miller's "Over the River" (April 1941). Told through the eyes of a vampire on the run, it gives the reader an insight into the degradation of such an existence.

Other vampire stories from the pulps for which I have space for only a brief mention are Robert Bloch's "Death is a Vampire" (*Thrilling Mystery*, September 1944), Manuel Komroff's "A Red Coat for Night" (*Argosy Magazine*, December 1944), George Whitley's "And Not in Peace" (*Famous Fantastic Mysteries*, December 1946), and William Tenn's "The Human Angle" (*Famous Fantastic Mysteries*, October 1948).

Writers contributing to the science fiction pulps of the forties also frequently utilized the vampire motif. Most of their stories were patterned on Eric Frank Russell's novel *Sinister Barrier*, which caused quite a stir when it appeared in the first issue of *Unknown*. Based on the intriguing notion that the Earth is secretly controlled by aliens, it speculated that the human race is the property of energy-vampires who feed on human emotions engendered by stressful situations. Globular in shape, but normally invisible to the human eye, their existence is detected when scientists develop new techniques in eye surgery which enables those who have been treated to see beyond the normal light spectrum.

Another famous story about alien vampires is A. E. van Vogt's "Asylum" (*Astounding Science-Fiction*, May 1942); and a remarkable assortment of vampires (mainly of the extraterrestrial kind) also appear in the following science fiction yarns: "Vampire of the Void" by Neil R. Jones (*Planet Stories*, Spring 1941), "Vampire Queen" by Thornton Ayre (*Planet Stories*, Fall 1942), "Stellar Vampires" by Frank B. Long (*Science Fiction Stories*, July 1943), and "The Chemical Vampire" by Lee Francis (*Amazing*, March 1949).

Two masterly vampire stories published in Ray Bradbury's first hardcover collection, *Dark Carnival* (1947), were "The Man Upstairs" and "Homecoming." Reprinted several times since, both reflect Bradbury's unique approach to the theme. In "The Man Upstairs" a young boy's curiosity is aroused by the odd behavior of his grandparents' new boarder, who always works evenings, is afraid of silver, and when looked at through colored glass has a disturbingly non-human appearance. The revelation that he is the vampire who has been terrifying the neighborhood comes to light at the story's gruesome conclusion, when the youngster sneaks into the stranger's room while he is asleep, calmly cuts him open, and removes his innards. In a relatively lighter vein, "Homecoming" focusses on the unhappiness of a 14-year-old boy, who regards himself as a misfit because the other members of his family are vampires.

Other outstanding vampire stories that achieved book publication in the United States in the 1940s were David H. Keller's "Heredity" (*Life Everlasting and Other Tales of Science, Fantasy & Horror*, 1947), Truman Capote's "Miriam" (*A Tree of Night & Other Stories*, 1949), and Fritz Leiber's "The Girl with the Hungry Eyes" (1949). In Keller's grim tale a businessman is murdered by his vampire wife and lycanthropic son; while Capote's rare excursion into the macabre revolves around the sinister activities of a little girl, who vampirically drains the will of a woman for whom she has formed a parasitic attachment. Deadlier still is the alluring vampire-woman in Leiber's powerful allegory of hucksterism, who demands literally everything from the men she seduces.

A few literate but rather dull vampire stories by British authors also found their way into print. They included H. T. W. Bousfield's "Death and the Duchess" (*Vinegar—and Cream*, 1941), M. P. Dare's "The Demoniac Goat" (*Unholy Relics & Other Uncanny Tales*, 1947), and Sir Andrew Caldecott's "Authorship Disputed" (*Fires Burn Blue*, 1948).

The steady decline in British weird fiction continued throughout the 1940s, reaching its lowest ebb in the immediate post-war years, when a coterie of Grub Street hacks were the only competition for the slick American material which was flooding the British market. The output of these fifth-raters was almost entirely published in cheap digest magazines put out by back-street publishers, who enjoyed a brief existence during the drab days of austerity and rationing. Among this plethora of trash are to be found the following vampire tales: "The Grey Beast" by Justin Atholl, "Spawn of the Vampire" by N. Wesley Firth, "The Vampire" by Leslie H. Fox, "Vampires Work at Night" by Shelley Smith, "Schloss Wappenburg" by D. Scott-Moncrieff, and "The Sadistic Vampire" and "Death of the Vampire Baroness" by Violet Van der Elst. More interesting than her insipid stories, Miss Van der Elst was a wealthy woman best-known in her day as a staunch campaigner against capital punishment, for which the Press dubbed her "The angel in a Rolls Royce."

The general public's disinterest in horror fiction around this time is reflected in the dearth of vampire novels. Two that did appear, Irina Karlova's *Dreadful Hollow* (1942) and Eugene Ascher's *There Were No Asper Ladies* (1944), are now deservedly forgotten.

A Change of Image

In the early 1950s, writers of weird fiction were finding fewer markets available for their stories. Most of the pulps had ceased publication by this time, and the digest-size magazines taking their place were strongly oriented towards science fiction, which was enjoying an unprecedented boom. *Weird Tales* struggled on for a while—even going over to a digest format—but finally had to admit defeat in 1954, the last issue appearing in September of that year.

Vampire stories published by "The Unique Magazine" in the four years prior to its demise included Margaret St. Clair's "The Family" (January 1950), Evangeline Walton's "At the End of the Corridor" (May 1950), Victoria Glad's "Each Man Kills" (March 1951), Roger M. Thomas's "The Bradley Vampire" (May 1951), Manly Wade Wellman's "The Last Grave of Lill Warran" (May 1951), Alvin Taylor and Len Moffatt's "Father's Vampire" (May 1952), and Thorp McClusky's "The Lamia in the Penthouse" (May 1952). Without exception, they were all run-of-the-mill, reflecting the mediocrity into which this once-great magazine had sunk.

With the dawning space-age opening up a new imaginative dimension, fantasy fiction underwent a dramatic change in the fifties. Shrouded ghosts and haunted castles were summarily banished from the pages of the "new-look" fantasy magazines, to be replaced by the ultra-modern paraphernalia of science fiction. The vampire, however, remained popular. Infinitely adaptable, it easily survived the transition, re-emerging in a host of new guises.

Among the stories reflecting this modernized image were C. M. Kornbluth's "The Mindworm" (*Worlds Beyond*, December 1950), Rog Phillips' "Vampires of the Deep" (*Amazing Stories*, May 1951), Damon Knight's "Eripmav" (*The Magazine of Fantasy & Science Fiction*, June 1958), Richard F. Watson's "Vampires from Outer Space" (*Super-Science Fiction*, April 1959), and Jack Douglas' "The Traitor" (*Amazing Stories*, July 1959). The bizarre assortment of vampires depicted in these stories included an emotion-sucking mutant ("The Mindworm") and a race of cellulose vampires ("Eripmav").

The science fiction magazines of the day also carried several "post-holocaust" stories revolving around the vampire's alleged indestructibility. In two that are fairly typical, Charles Beaumont's "Place of Meeting" (*Orbit*, January 1953) and Joe Hensley's "And Not Quite Human" (*Beyond*, September 1953), a handful of vampires are the only survivors of a global catastrophe; while a solitary vampire finds himself in a similar predicament in Theodore Cogswell's "The Masters" (*Thrilling Wonder*, Summer 1954).

The first novel to offer a credible pseudo-scientific explanation of vampirism was *I Am Legend* (1954) by Richard Matheson. An apocalyptic nightmare with political overtones, it relates the story of Robert Neville, the only man on earth immune to a bacterial plague that has killed millions of people and turned the remainder into zombie-like vampires.

Fearing for his safety, Neville seeks refuge in a barricaded house, keeping his former friends and neighbors at bay with sprigs of garlic and other traditional vampire repellents. In the daytime, when the vampires are inactive he ventures out and exterminates all those he can find; the rest of his time is spent investigating the cause of the disease that has destroyed civilization.

After many trials and tribulations, Neville makes contact with a group of infected people who have found a way to neutralize the effect of the bacillus, and as a result are able to lead near-normal lives. Ironically, Neville's hopes that he might find sanctuary among them are dashed when he learns from the group leaders that they plan to establish a new society in which there will be no place for anyone not like themselves. This involves not only the systematic destruction of the vampires, but Neville, as the last of the old race, must forfeit his life too.

Matheson has also written several short stories with a vampire element. In one of the best-known, "No Such Thing as a Vampire" (1959), a cuckolded husband takes a fiendish revenge on his wife's lover. Secretly extracting small quantities of the unfaithful woman's blood to make it look like she is the victim of a vampire, he cunningly arranges it so his rival gets the blame. Two other stories by Matheson which brought a new twist to the vampire theme were "Drink My Red Blood" (*Imagination*, April 1951) and "Dress of White Silk" (*The Magazine of Fantasy & Science Fiction*, October 1951). Both stories concern children who behave abnormally: in the former a small boy is consumed with a burning desire to become one of the Undead; and in the latter a little girl commits acts of vampirism after trying on her dead mother's dress.

Another leading American author who purposely avoided plot clichés traditionally associated with the vampire was Robert Bloch. Two offbeat stories that resulted from this policy were "I Kiss Your Shadow" (*The Magazine of Fantasy & Science Fiction*, April 1956), which gave an unusual twist to the succubus motif, and "Dig That Crazy Grave!" (*Ellery Queen's Mystery Magazine*, June 1957), in which a band of jazz musicians stay ever-young by vampirizing their fans.

Typical of the witty stories with a sting in the tail that Bloch favored during this decade is the black comedy "Hungarian Rhapsody." Originally published under his "Wilson Kane" pseudonym in the June 1958 issue of *Fantastic*, it is probably best remembered for the titillating scene where the sexy vampiress, lying on a bed strewn with her native soil, voluptuously caresses her naked body with gold coins. This was one of two stories by Bloch in this particular issue of *Fantastic*; the other—quite different—was "Terror in Cut-Throat Cove", a sensational Cthulhu Mythos yarn about a gigantic squid-like deity that preys on divers searching for sunken treasure. The monster's victims are devoured through lidded mouths resembling eyes, and their decapitated heads subsequently appear on the end of its writhing tentacles. Indestructible and irresistible, the vampire-god incorporates its victims' essence into itself, adding their thoughts, emotions, knowledge, etc. to its own. After each feast it increases in size and power, ultimately posing a threat to all life on earth.

Several stories by other popular contributors to American fantasy magazines of the fifties display a similar freshness in their approach to the vampire theme. Notable for its wry humor and clever twist ending is Fredric Brown's "Blood" (*The Magazine of Fantasy & Science Fiction*, February 1955), in which the last two vampires on earth escape into the future in a time machine, only to find that all life-forms from which they can extract nourishment have become extinct. In Philip K. Dick's "The Cookie Lady" (*Fantasy Magazine*, June 1953) the vampire is a kindly old woman, who becomes young and vital again after unwittingly draining the energy of a greedy little boy; and in William Tenn's "She Only Goes Out at Night" (*Fantastic Universe Magazine*, October 1956) a young vampiress who has fallen in love with one of her intended victims is restored to normality when it is discovered that her condition is caused by a metabolic deficiency. Love also triumphs over evil in James Hart's "The Traitor" (*The Magazine of Fantasy & Science Fiction*, Fall 1950). Here a vampire posing as a socialite turns against his own kind when he falls for a lovely young woman he meets at a dinner party. Similar touches of originality are to be found in August Derleth's "Who Shall I Say is Calling?" (*The Magazine of Fantasy & Science Fiction*, August 1952), Jerome Bixby and Joe E. Dean's "Share Alike" (*Beyond*, July 1953), Charles E. Fritch's "Much Ado About Plenty" (*Fantasy Magazine*, August 1953), Colin Cassidy's "Revenge of the Jukebox Vampire" (*Monster Parade*, September 1958), and Lawrence Block's "I'll Love You to Death!" (*Monster Parade*, September 1958).

American vampire stories from other sources included "The Music" by Theodore Sturgeon (*E Pluribus Unicorn*, 1953), "One Man's Meat" by Vince Greene (*Anthology of Best Original Short-Stories*, 1955), "The Hunt" by Joseph Payne Brennan (*Nine Horrors and a Dream*, 1958), and "My Lips Destroy" by Cornell Woolrich (*Beyond the Night*, 1959).

The only British vampire stories of any consequence dating from this era are Robert Aickman's "Insufficient Answer" (1951), John Wyndham's "Close Behind Him" (*Fantastic*, February 1953), and E. C. Tubb's "Fresh Guy" (*Science Fantasy*, June 1958). A short novel also worth noting is *The Feasting Dead* (1954) by John Metcalfe, which centers on the strange bond between an English schoolboy and a vampiric revenant.

The Vampire Revival

In the early 1960s the craze for horror movies—especially those featuring vampires—gave rise to a corresponding upsurge in horror fiction. Inevitably, vampire novels were to the forefront in popularity, and by the end of the decade the number flowing off the presses had grown into a veritable flood. More literary than most were Theodore Sturgeon's *Some of Your Blood* (1961) and Ray Bradbury's *Something Wicked This Way Comes* (1962). The former tells the story of an orphaned youth who feeds exclusively on menstrual blood, whilst the latter has a heavily symbolic vampire element.

Minor novels from the same decade include *The Man Who Made Maniacs* (1961) by Jim Harmon, *The Shiny Narrow Grin* (1964) by Jane Gaskell, *Progeny of the Adder* (1965) by Leslie H. Whitten, *So What Killed the Vampire?* (1966) by Carter Brown, *Thorns* (1967) by Robert Silverberg, *The Torturer* (1967) by Peter Saxon, *The Vampire Cameo* (1968) by Dorothea Nile, *The Orgy at Madame Dracula's* (1968) by F. W. Paul, *Secret of the Pale Lover* (1969) by Clarissa Ross, and *Night of the Vampire* (1969) by Raymond Giles.

Robert Bloch's major contribution to the vampire canon in the sixties was a short story called "The Living Dead" (1967), in which an actor who plays the part of a vampire too well ends up having a stake driven through his heart. Another former *Weird Tales* author, Joseph Payne Brennan, penned a story called "The Vampire Bat" (*Scream at Midnight*, 1963), and British author Michael Harrison included "The Vampire of the Rue du Bouloy" in his Arkham House collection *The Exploits of the Chevalier Dupin* (1968). Around the same time the former executive editor of *Playboy Magazine*, Ray Russell, surprised everybody by producing three well-crafted novellas in the Gothic tradition (collected in *Unholy Trinity*, 1967), two of which, "Sagittarius" and "Sanguinarius," had a vampire motif. In "Sagittarius," Gilles de Rais has survived down the centuries and is carrying on his vampirish activities in 19th-century Paris, where he leads a double life, alternating between two assumed identities: Sellig, a handsome classical actor, and Laval, the facially disfigured star performer with the Grand Guignol theater. "Sanguinarius," set in 17th-century Hungary, features an equally famous historical figure, Elizabeth Bathory. Russell, however, has done a highly effective whitewash job on the vampiric countess, who is presented in a most sympathetic light as the unwitting dupe of her evil husband and his mistress.

Russell's vignette "The Exploits of Argo" (1961) is in a lighter vein. Set in the far future, it tells of the ironic fate of the deposed Emperor of the Asteroids, who becomes a were-vampire on a planet totally unsuited to his special needs. There is an equally clever twist in the tail to a short story by Charles Beaumont called "Blood Brother" (1963), in which a reluctant vampire consults a psychiatrist about his problem, and gets the sort of treatment he hadn't bargained for—a knife through the heart! Richard A. Johnstone also parodied the theme in a spoof called "Mr. Alucard" (1964), and Thomas M. Disch joined in the fun with a side-splitting send-up titled "The Vamp" (1965).

Several notable vampire stories appeared in leading fantasy magazines of the day. These included Evelyn E. Smith's "Softly While You're Sleeping" (*The Magazine of Fantasy & Science Fiction.* April 1961), A. E. van Vogt's "The Proxy Intelligence" (*If*, December 1968), and Fritz Leiber's "Ship of Shadows" (*The Magazine of Fantasy & Science Fiction*, July 1969), which received the prestigious Hugo award. A noted vampire story from 1930 which turned up again in the May 1968 issue of *Fantastic* was Kathleen Ludwick's "Dr. Immortelle"; and twenty-seven years after its aborted serialization in the short-lived *Marvel Tales*, the August 1962 issue of *Fantastic* carried the full, unexpurgated version of P. Schuyler Miller's novelette "The Titan." Set on Mars, where the ruling class are sustained by a form of institutionalized vampirism, it was originally considered too erotic for mass publication.

Although fantasy magazines remained the main market for weird fiction they were increasingly becoming something of a publishing liability, and not many of the new titles launched during the sixties survived beyond the first few issues. Two that lasted longer than most were *Magazine of Horror* (1963-71) and *Startling Mystery Stories* (1966-1971), both edited by Robert A. W. Lowndes. Early issues contained mainly reprints from the pulps (*Strange Tales* was a popular source); but as the magazines became established, up-and-coming writers were given a chance to make their mark.

In *Magazine of Horror* the best of these newcomers was Steffan B. Aletti. Among the handful of short stories he contributed to the magazine was an eerie vampire tale, "The Last Work of Pietro of Apono." Featured in the May 1969 issue, it tells how a young student foolishly performs a magical rite to conjure up a vampiric demon, and is forced to commit suicide to save his soul. In *Startling Mystery Stories* the pick of the vampire stories were Dona Tolson's "Nice Old House" (Winter 1967/68), in which the new tenant of a spooky old house is devoured by a vampire-sofa, and Dorothy Norman Cooke's "The Parasite" (Winter 1969), a gruesome variation on the seemingly inexhaustible theme of bloodsucking plants.

The tally of vampire stories from fantasy magazines published in the sixties and early seventies also includes "The Arrogant Vampire" by Arthur Porges (*Fantastic*, May 1961); "The Vampire was a Sucker" by 'Siral' (*Thriller*, February 1962); "The Stainless Steel Leech" by Harrison Denmark (*Amazing Stories*, April 1963); "Food" by Ray Nelson (*Gamma*, February 1965); "The Tree" by Gerald W. Page (*Magazine of Horror*, August 1965); "Count Down to Doom" by Charles Nuetzel and Viktor Vesperto (*Monster World*, No. 8, May 1966); "The Gates" by Walter Quednau (*Weirdbook*, April 1968); "Death is a Lonely Place" by Bill Warren (*Worlds of Fantasy*, September 1968); "Dr. Adams' Garden of Evil" by Fritz Leiber (*Strange Fantasy*, Spring 1969); "Odile" by Alan Caillou (*Coven 13*, September 1969); "The Girl in 218" by Laurence R. Griffin (*Macabre*, February 1970); "I, Vampire!" by Bill Pronzini and Jeffrey Wallman (*Coven 13*, March 1970); "High Moon" by Gregory Francis (*Weirdbook*, January 1971); "Sleep Well, Teresa" by James R. Hillyer (*Weirdbook*, February 1972); "Experiment" by Othello F. Peters (*Moonbroth*, No. 5, 1972); "In the Sorcerer's Garden" by Susan M. Patrick (*Witchcraft & Sorcery*, Winter 1972); "Thirst" by Gerald W. Page (*Witchcraft & Sorcery*, Winter 1972); and "Hard Times" by Sonora Morrow (*Ellery Queen's Mystery Magazine*, December 1974).

In the early 1970s, *Adventures in Horror*, a sensational magazine offering the questionable novelty of semi-pornographic horror fiction briefly found its way onto the newsstands. It tempted the reader with salaciously-titled stories, all of which were a sordid mixture of sex and sadism. Vampire stories from its "sin-packed" pages include "Love is the Color of Blood" by J. P. Tarleton (October 1970); "Trapped in the Vampire's Web of Icy Death" by Harlan Williams (December 1970); "The

Vampire's Fangs Were Red with My Woman's Blood" by Andrew Palmer (February 1971); "Feast of Blood for the Girl who Couldn't Die" by Martha Scott (April 1971); "Feast of Blood in the House of the Vampire" by Henry Lawes (June 1971); "Fangs of the Fiend for the Girl who Died Twice" by Obadiah Kemp (August 1971); "Shrieking Victim of the Vampire's Curse" by William Arnes (October 1971). Three similar stories, "Castle Dracula" by Chester Winfield, "The Voyage of Dracula" by Roy Hemp, and "Lust of the Vampire" by Dudley McDonley, were published in a sleazy magazine called *Monster Sex Tales*, which was dated August/ September 1972.

Of more significance during this period was the renewed interest in macabre verse, the bulk of which appeared in small press publications and fan journals. Vampire poems from these sources included "Morning of the Vampire" by Elizabeth Weistrop (*Macabre*, Winter 1964/65); "Vampire" by William J. Noble (*Macabre*, No. 20, 1968); "Love Philter" by H. Warner Munn (*Weirdbook*, April 1968); "The Vampire's Tryst" by Wade Wellman (*Arkham Collector*, Summer 1968); "To His Mistress, Dead and Darkly Return'd" by Roger Johnson (*Arkham Collector*, Winter 1971); "The Onlooker" by Wade Wellman (*Arkham Collector*, Summer 1969); "Vampiric Madness" by Lewis Sanders (*Moonbroth*, No. 15, 1974); "Night Visitant" by Richard L. Tierney (*Whispers*, November 1974); "Nosferatu" by G. Sutton Breiding (*Moonbroth*, No. 21, 1975); "Black Leather Vampire" by Bill Breiding (*Moonbroth*, No. 23, 1976); "Vampyre" by Susan Tannahill (*Moonbroth*, No. 25, 1976); "The Vampire" by Edith Ogutsch (*Escape!*, Fall 1977); "The Vampires" by Mark McLaughlin (*The Diversifier*, February/March 1979); "Apprentice Vampire" by Arthur Griffin (*Weirdbook*, June 1979); and many more.

While all this was going on in the United States, a similar resurgence of interest in the vampire story was taking place in Great Britain and other European countries with a tradition of weird literature. The main market for British horror stories during the sixties and early seventies were paperback anthologies, especially the long-running *Pan Book of Horror Stories* series, which, since its inception in 1959, has been regularly criticized for the preponderance of stories depicting obscene acts of physical cruelty. The relatively few vampire stories that have found their way into these books are certainly not for the squeamish. Particularly nauseating are Charles Lloyd's "Special Diet" (Book 3, 1962), Martin Waddell's "Bloodthirsty" (Book 9, 1968), Lindsey Stewart's "Jolly Uncle" (Book 9, 1968), Gerald Atkins' "The Midnight Lover" (Book 11, 1970), and Morag Greer's "Under the Flagstone" (Book 15, 1974). More restrained is Dulcie Gray's "The Fur Brooch" (Book 7, 1966), in which the bloodsucking is done by a beetle set in a piece of jewelry.

On a higher level are the horror stories of Ronald Chetwynd-Hayes, who in recent years has emerged as a prolific spinner of vampire yarns. One of the best-known, "The Door" (*Cold Terror*, 1973), has a characteristically ingenious plot. Following the demolition of a sixteenth-century manor-house, the antique door to one of the rooms is acquired by a writer, who has it fitted to a cupboard in his study. Over the ensuing weeks he becomes obsessed with the door's history, and through the agency of a dream discovers that it is a trap created by an undead sorcerer. Active at certain times, the treacherous portal lures people into the ghost-room beyond its threshold, where they end up as sacrifices, their life-essence perpetuating the existence of the room and its evil creator. In a thrilling climax the sorcerer and the vampire-room are simultaneously destroyed when the door is hacked to pieces.

A further three gripping vampire tales by same author, "The Labyrinth," "Birth," and "Jumpity-Jim," were included in a collection titled *The Elemental* (1974). In "The Labyrinth" a sinister country-house is an extension of the personality of a 500-year-old vampire buried beneath the foundations. Travelers invited inside the forbidding edifice are lured through a great mouth-like door set in the wall of the dining room; and once trapped inside the maze of corridors on the other side are gradually drained of their vital essences. In "Birth," a man struck down by a fatal heart attack uses his willpower to survive death. Still able to think, even though he is now a disembodied spirit, it occurs to him that his home has become saturated with his personality over the years, and by molding his thoughts into tubes he can suck in the wastage of his soul and create a new body for himself. The snag is that after his rematerialization is successfully accomplished the man develops vampiric tendencies, and ends up killing his wife and draining her body of blood. Vampirism of a very different sort figures in "Jumpity-Jim." Here the supernatural menace is provided by a loathsome elemental which feeds on life-essence and warm blood. Popularly known as a jumpity-jim, because of its ability to leap about with prodigious speed and agility, it is described as a cross between a deformed monkey and a monstrous spider. Once raised by a sorcerer, it seeks out a virgin who has the right essence, and should the flesh of her back be bare it leaps upon it and fastens itself there like a grotesque hump. A permanent fixture from then on, the demon cannot be removed unless another virgin cursed with the same essence can be induced, or forced, to accept the hideous burden.

Chetwynd-Hayes' tally of vampire stories also includes "Looking for Something to Suck" (*The Fourth Fontana Book of Great Horror Stories*, 1969), "Great-Grandad Walks Again" (*Cold Terror*, 1973), "My Mother Married a Vampire" (*The Cradle Demon & Other Stories*, 1975), "The Holstein Horror" (*The Night Ghouls*, 1975), and "Amelia" (*The Fantastic World of Kamtellar*, 1980).

Good though most of the aforementioned are, the story that is generally regarded as the finest contribution to the vampire canon made by a British author in the 1970s is the late Robert Aickman's "Pages from a Young Girl's Journal" (1972), which won the 1975 World Fantasy Award for Best Short Fiction. Set in the 19th century, it is narrated by a young Englishwoman who falls under the spell of a Byronic vampire while touring the Continent with her parents. Fully aware of the inevitable outcome of such a relationship she confides to her diary: "How I rejoice when I think about the new life which spreads before me into infinity. Soon, soon, new force will be mine, fire that is inconceivable; and the power to assume any night-shape that I may wish, or to fly through the darkness with none." About her lover she rapturously declares: "What love is his! How chosen among all women am I."

The most controversial vampire story produced by a British author in the seventies was undoubtedly Ken Cowley's "Dracula Reflects" (1978), which builds up to the astounding revelation that the Count is really Jesus Christ. Two other unorthodox interpretations of the theme were Brian Lumley's "Haggopian" (1973), in which a world-famous ichthyologist forms a symbiotic relationship with a bloodsucking fish, and Tanith Lee's "Red as Blood" (1979), which raised a few eyebrows by introducing a vampire element into the Snow White fairytale. Four stories with a more traditional flavor, "Domdaniel" by Peter Allan, "To Claim His Own" by Crispen Derby, "Dies Irae" by Richard Howard, and "Mirror Without Image" by James Turner, were included in Peter Underwood's fact and fiction compilation *The Vampire's Bedside Companion* (1975).

Vampire novels by British authors also began to appear more frequently in the 1970s, thanks largely to New English Library's promotion of new talent in their series of paperback horror novels. Typical of the sort of fare that appeared under this imprint was Errol Lecale's

The Death Box (1974), which featured an occult detective called "The Specialist." His adversary is a vampiric nobleman called Dagmar the Black, who is able to enlist the aid of a pack of spectral hounds from the Twilight World, who prey on human souls. The high point of the narrative is the climactic duel between Dagmar and the psychic sleuth, which is fought out on two planes, the astral as well as the physical. A subsequent novel about "The Specialist," *Blood of My Blood* (1975), also utilized the vampire theme, but lacked the inventiveness of its predecessor.

In another entertaining entry in the series, Brian Ball's *The Venomous Serpent* (1974), the focus of horror is a brass rubbing. Taken from a brass in a village church, it depicts a notorious medieval sorceress and her dog-like familiar. One night the vampiric duo are aroused from death by the moonlight shining on the rubbing, and thereafter terrorize the local community. At first the evil pair are restricted to drinking the blood of small animals, but once fully materialized are able to batten onto human victims, who subsequently join the ranks of the Undead.

Similar touches of originality are also evident in some of the other vampire novels published by New English Library. Those from the seventies include George Charles Clewett's *Blood Dynasty* (1973), Ian Dear's *The Village of Blood* (1974), Etienne Aubin's *Dracula and the Virgins of the Undead* (1974), Louise Cooper's *Blood Summer* (1976) and *In Memory of Sarah Bailey* (1977), and Guy N. Smith's *Bats Out of Hell* (1979).

The increased output of vampire stories and novels from British fantasists was, to a lesser degree, emulated by their counterparts on the European continent. Leading the way was the multilingual Belgian author Eddy C. Bertin, whose highly original treatments of the theme included "The Whispering Horror" (*The Ninth Pan Book of Horror Stories*, 1968), "Now You May Kiss Me, Honey" (*Vampire, Vampire, Take Another Bite on Me*, 1972), "The Price to Pay" (*Fantasy Tales*, Summer 1977), and "Something Small, Something Hungry" (*Weirdbook*, May 1978). This last story, in which a series of fatal accidents at a circus are caused by a vampiric fetus, was later expanded into a full-length novel entitled *Circus of Darkness*.

Many other short stories and novels by contemporary European fantasy writers could also be cited, but unfortunately the lack of English translations precludes their inclusion in this survey.

Beyond the Tomb

Although many of the great names from the golden age of American weird fiction are now deceased, their influence continues to be felt. This is particularly so in the case of H. P. Lovecraft, whose famous myth-pattern, the Cthulhu Mythos, has been borrowed and extensively expanded by his latter-day disciples.

As is well-known to devotees of Lovecraft's fiction, the prime postulate of his Cthulhu Mythos stories is that there exist gates to and from other dimensions through which powerful non-human forces inimical to mankind are attempting to gain a footing on Earth. Behind this recurrent theme lies the supposition that our planet had once been ruled by anarchic entities who crossed the Void from other universes incalculable eons ago; and that termination of their reign occurred when they were expelled by superior forces allied to the cause of Order and the laws of the cosmos.

The defeated gods were subsequently dispersed to different parts of the Void, from where they ceaselessly plot to regain their former domain, using as tools a handful of mad experimenters and "sensitives" living in the world today, who are insane or misguided enough to unseal the gates that bar their entry. Aggressively hungry, these undying monstrosities absorb any living thing that comes within their sphere of sensation, and despite the hideousness of their appearance have a fatal attraction which compels those who serve them to ultimately sacrifice their personal identity and become one with them.

In the original stories by Lovecraft the vampiric nature of The Great Old Ones and their minions was never given much importance, but latterly his acolytes have brought it more to the fore. For instance, in Ramsey Campbell's "The Insects from Shaggai" (*The Inhabitant of the Lake and Less Welcome Tenants*, 1964) the narrator of the story has his mind taken over by a vampiric entity from another dimension; and in Walter C. DeBill's "Where Yidhra Walks" (*The Disciples of Cthulhu*, 1976) an eon-old, multi-bodied macro-organism is sustained by the life essences of its followers scattered about the globe. Another of Lovecraft's imitators, Brian Lumley, has written about strange, worm-like vampires in "Cement Surroundings" (*Tales of the Cthulhu Mythos*, 1969); and in another of his Mythos stories, "The House of the Temple" (*Weird Tales 3*, 1981), there is a pool-dwelling monster which sucks out men's souls. Colin Wilson's contributions to this fascinating body of fiction include a full-length novel, *The Mind Parasites* (1967), and a short novel,

The Return of the Lloigor (1969), both of which concern vampires from outer space. Malignant extraterrestrials are also the villains of the piece in Wilson's non-Cthulhuoid novel *The Space Vampires* (1976). Here the threat to human survival is posed by energy vampires from a remote planet hundreds of light years from Earth. Squid-like in appearance, the alien invaders have highly developed brains and nervous systems, and can project their minds into the bodies of their victims.

Another long-deceased pulp-fiction writer who has been a major influence on contemporary fantasists is Robert E. Howard. One of the original "Three Musketeers" of *Weird Tales* (Lovecraft and C. A. Smith being the other two), he is best-remembered as the founder of the fantasy subgenre known as sword and sorcery. In stories belonging to this category, vampirism is only occasionally the main motif; usually a vampire in a suitably exotic guise is introduced into the plot as one of several supernatural forces menacing the hero.

Foremost among Howard's many imitators is the prolific American fantasist, Lin Carter, whose novels about Thongor, the mighty warrior-king of Lemuria, have featured a variety of vampires. More importantly, Carter (in collaboration with L. Sprague de Camp) has written a number of Howardian pastiches for the best-selling "Conan" paperback collections. Those with a vampire theme include "The Hand of Nergal" (*Conan*, 1967), "The Road of the Eagles" (*Conan the Freebooter*, 1968), "Black Tears" (*Conan the Wanderer*, 1968), and "The Castle of Terror" (*Conan of Cimmeria*, 1969).

In "Black Tears," which is arguably the best of the four stories, Conan is taken prisoner in a hostile desert region and forcibly brought before its despotic ruler, a Gorgon-like goddess with a third eye in her forehead, who turns people into stone prior to draining their life essence. Conan learns that many ages ago this vampiric deity had been summoned from the Death Dimension by a wicked sorcerer to rule over the region, and ever since has leeched the vitality from the population. A non-corporeal being, her flesh is composed merely of matter drawn to her and held together by her seemingly unconquerable will. But before the goddess can work her sorcery on Conan he destroys her power by thrusting his sword through her third eye, after which she turns into a wizened old hag and finally crumbles into dust.

An English author closely associated with the heroic fantasy novel is Michael Moorcock. In the early 1960s he created a strange, introverted hero called Elric of Melnibone, who owes all his strength and fighting prowess to his vampirous sword, Stormbringer. Possessing a life and intelligence of its own, the evil blade consumes the souls of those it slays in battle, and passes some of the stolen life-force onto the congenitally-weak Elric, transforming him into an invincible warrior.

More recently, in *The Swordbearer* (1982), Glen Cook introduced an Elric-like hero called Gathrid. Similarly cursed with the burden of a soul-drinking sword, he gets progressively stronger by assimilating the psyche and memories of his slain adversaries, who live on as actual personalities inside him.

Other sword-and-sorcery novels in which vampirism plays a significant part are Henry Kuttner's *The Dark World* (first book publication 1965), John Jakes' *Brak versus the Mark of the Demons* (1969), David Mason's *The Sorcerer's Skull* (1970), and Andrew J. Offutt and Richard Lyon's *The Demon in the Mirror* (1985). One of the co-authors of this last novel, Andrew J. Offutt, also edited an anthology of sword-and-sorcery stories called *Swords Against Darkness III* (1978), which contained four vampire yarns, "The Pit of Wings" by Ramsey Campbell, "Servitude" by Wayne Hooks, "Tower of Darkness" by David Madison, and "The Guest of Dzinganji" by Manly Wade Wellman. Hooks' story is something of a novelty, as the vampirizing (of the psychic kind) is done by a jewelled armlet worn by the hunchbacked hero.

Vampirism also plays an important part in Roger Zelazny's science-fantasy novel *Jack of Shadows* (1971). Deriving his strength from shadows, the roguish hero is able to wriggle his way out of the trickiest situations. At one point in the story, for example, he is attacked by a female vampire, but turns the tables on his assailant and proceeds to suck *her* blood. He also needs all his guile when he encounters a huge mossy boulder lying in the center of a barren circle eighty feet in diameter. Belying its innocuous appearance, it is really a malevolently animate stone vampire which can communicate with its intended victims by telepathy. Drawing Jack towards itself by hypnotic suggestion, it tells him: "I am the stone that gets blood from men." But Jack is too wily to be caught, and striking a light to create a shadow quickly reverses the roles of vampire and victim.

The Book of the Film

It has long been a common practice of film companies to buy the rights to best-selling novels for subsequent adaptation to the screen. In recent years, however, the trend has been reversed, and one now finds on the paperback bookshelves an increasing number of novels based on the screenplays of successful films, with a blurb on the cover proclaiming "The Book of the Film." In the horror category the most popular have been the novelizations of vampire movies, of which the following are a sample: *Dracula* (1960) by Russ Jones; *The Brides of Dracula* (1960) by Dean Owen; *Blood and Roses* (1960) by Robin Carlisle; *Queen of Blood* (1966) by Charles Nuetzel; *Dracula: Prince of Darkness* (1967) by John Burke; *The Scars of Dracula* (1971) by Angus Hall; *Countess Dracula* (1971) by Michel Parry; *Lust for a Vampire* (1971) by William Hughes; *Kronos* (1972) by Hugh Enfield; *The Werewolf vs. the Vampire Woman* (1972) by Arthur N. Scram; *Martin* (1977) by George Romero and Susan Sparrow; *Dracula's Daughter* (1977) by Carl Dreadstone (pseud. of Ramsey Campbell); *Zoltan, Hound of Dracula* (1977) by Ken Johnson; *Nosferatu: the Vampyre* (1979) by Paul Monette; *Fade to Black* (1980) by Ron Renauld; *Dracula Sucks* (1981) by Maxwell Kearny.

A string of paperback novels were similarly generated by the long-running television series *Dark Shadows* (1968-1971), all churned out with amazing rapidity by Dan Ross, who hid his true gender behind the pen-name of Marilyn Ross. Vapid Gothic romances aimed primarily at women readers, these novels nearly all featured a sympathetic vampire called Barnabas Collins, who was introduced into the series in the sixth novel, *Barnabas Collins* (1968). The remaining titles in the series, in which the refined, distinguished-looking vampire is pitted against an assortment of villains and supernatural phenomena, are *The Secret of Barnabas Collins* (1969), *The Demon of Barnabas Collins* (1969), *The Foe of Barnabas Collins* (1969), *The Phantom of Barnabas Collins* (1969), *Barnabas Collins versus the Warlock* (1969), *The Peril of Barnabas Collins* (1969), *Barnabas Collins and the Mysterious Ghost* (1969), *Barnabas Collins and the Gypsy Witch* (1969). A werewolf character called Quentin was then introduced, hence: *Barnabas Collins and Quentin's Demon* (1969), *Barnabas, Quentin and the Mummy's Curse* (1970), *Barnabas, Quentin and the Avenging Ghost* (1970), *Barnabas, Quentin and the Nightmare Assassin* (1970), *Barnabas, Quentin and the Crystal Coffin* (1970), *Barnabas, Quentin and the Witch's Curse* (1970), *Barnabas, Quentin and the Haunted Cave* (1970), *Barnabas, Quentin and the Frightened Bride* (1970), *Barnabas, Quentin and the Scorpio Curse* (1970), *Barnabas, Quentin and the Serpent* (1970), *Barnabas, Quentin and the Magic Potion* (1970), *Barnabas, Quentin and the Body Snatchers* (1971), *Barnabas, Quentin and Dr. Jekyll's Son* (1971), *Barnabas, Quentin and the Grave Robbers* (1971), *Barnabas, Quentin and the Sea Ghost* (1971), *Barnabas, Quentin and the Mad Magician* (1971), *Barnabas, Quentin and the Hidden Tomb* (1971), *Barnabas, Quentin and the Vampire Beauty* (1972). Also by the same author, but independent of the series, is *The House of Dark Shadows* (1970), which is based on the movie of the same name.

The show's still-active fan organization has also published a considerable amount of fiction. Fan-produced "Dark Shadows" novels include *Dark Angel* (1977) and *Dark Lord* (1980) by Jean Graham; *No Other Love* (1978) by Judy Zachery; *Paradox* (1979) by Kathy Resch; *Resolutions in Time* (1980) by Dale Clark; *Tryst of Dark Shadows* (1981) by Beth Tignor; and *A Twist of Mind* (1981) by Lucille Staszak. Additionally, the leading DS fanzine, *The World of Dark Shadows*, has published the following short stories: "Kitt's Choice" by Kathy Resch (*WofDS* 1, November 1975), "The Taste of Death" by Marcy Robin (*WofDS* 9, February 1977), "The Unending Night" by Dee L. Gurnett (*WofDS* 11, June 1977), "In the Light of a Candle" by Marcy Robin (*WofDS* 13, October 1977), "Purgatory" by Marcy Robin (*WofDS* 16-17, May 1978), "Surrounded by Dark Shadows" by Jeff Arsenhault (*WofDS* 18, June 1978), "Cursed" by Marcy Robin (*WofDS* 19, July 1978), "Home to Collinwood" by Sandy Smith (*WofDS* 19, July 1978), "Paradox Lost" by Jean Lorrah (*WofDS* 20-21, March 1979), "The Final Truth" by Marcy Robin (*WofDS* 24-25, February 1980), "Blood in the Night" by Jeff Arsenhault and Kathy Resch (*WofDS* 28, February 1981), "The Stranger" by Jane Lach (*WofDS* 28, February 1981), "Come Join Me in Death" by Theresa Mudryk (*WofDS* 30, July 1982), and "Whence No Man Steers" by Virginia Waldron (*WofDS* 30, July 1982).

"Dark Shadows" stories have also been included in several anthologies. "Edge" by Kathy Resch, along with four stories by Marcy Robin, "Farewell Memories," "The Time for Grief," "Transition," and "Premonition," were included in *Decades* (1977), edited by Kathy Resch; "Eternity Now" by Marcy Robin was among the stories in *Dark Fires: Impressions from Dark Shadows* (1980), edited by Edlyne Bond; and "Web" by Peter Reeves and "Shadowed Soul" by the ubiquitous Marcy Robin appeared in *Chosen Haunts* (1981), edited by William Hunt.

Tied in with another popular TV program of yesteryear is *The Vampire Affair* (1966) by David McDaniel, one of a string of novels based on The Man from U.N.C.L.E. series. Similarly, *The Night Stalker* (1973) by Jeff Rice is based on the enormously successful TV-movie of the same name, in which a brash newspaper reporter assigned to cover a series of bizarre murders in Las Vegas discovers they are the work of a vampire, but has difficulty in getting the authorities to believe him.

The Return of Dracula

As every horror fans knows, Count Dracula's evil existence was terminated in the final chapter of Bram Stoker's famous thriller; but latterly the arch-vampire has been resurrected and given a new lease of life in a spate of cheap paperback novels, most of which have been written by a small band of hacks out to make a fast buck by cashing in on the selling power of the character's charismatic name. Of these "new" Dracula novels the most banal have been those in "The Dracula Horror Series" by Robert Lory. *Dracula Returns!* launched the series in 1973, and a further eight novels followed in quick succession. Primarily aimed at the juvenile market, the remaining titles in the series are *The Hand of Dracula, Dracula's Brothers, Dracula's Gold, The Drums of Dracula, The Witching of Dracula, Dracula's Lost World, Dracula's Disciple,* and *Challenge to Dracula.*

More adult are those Dracula novels that have imitated the style and format of the original, using extracts from letters, diaries, etc. as a frame. Raymond Rudorff set the ball rolling in 1971 with a well-researched novel, *The Dracula Archives,* which put the Dracula legend into a historical perspective by ingeniously fabricating a family connection between the real-life Vlad Dracula and the purely fictional Count Dracula.

Alternative accounts of how the "historical" Dracula became a vampire are given in Gail Kimberly's *Dracula Began* (1976) and Peter Tremayne's *Dracula Unborn* (1977). Although it probably fooled nobody, the latter purported to be an historical document written by Vlad Tepes' son (hence its American title: *Bloodright: Memoirs of Mircea, Son to Dracula*). Not steeped in evil like the rest of his family, Mircea finds himself drawn into a life-or-death struggle with his vampiric father and brothers when they try to force him to become one of them. In two subsequent novels, *The Revenge of Dracula* (1978) and *Dracula, My Love* (1980), Tremayne kept much closer to Stoker's characterization. In *Revenge,* Dracula is described as a descendent of the followers of the ancient Egyptian cult of Draco, whose priests discovered how to make the body immortal five thousand years ago. Dissatisfied with the limited powers his present existence offers, Dracula sets about perfecting a magical ritual which will give him the true immortality of a god; but in the nick of time his plans for world domination are thwarted by the hero. The third novel in the trilogy, *Dracula, My Love*, shows the arch-vampire in a much more sympathetic light. Here a young, destitute Scots lass is forced to accept the post of governess at Castle Dracula, and then gradually finds herself becoming emotionally involved with the Count, who for once shows that he is capable of love. Ultimately the girl is faced with the choice of either destroying her demon lover or sharing his life for eternity.

Fred Saberhagen's controversial "New Dracula" novels have revamped the Count's image even more drastically, changing him from a villain into a hero. The first volume in the series, *The Dracula Tape* (1975), is a rebuttal of Stoker's novel, retelling it, scene for scene, from the vampire's perspective. To put the record straight, Dracula tracks down the descendents of Mina and Jonathan Harker, and insists on the couple listening to a tape-recording on which he attempts to correct the public's image of him as a monster, giving an alternate explanation for everything that happened during his trip to England in 1891.

In the equally sensational sequel, *The Holmes-Dracula File* (1978), the reader is asked to believe that Sherlock Holmes is Count Dracula's half nephew. To explain this hitherto unsuspected relationship it is alleged that the great detective's mother was a lady of loose morals who mated with Dracula's younger brother during a trip to Switzerland, the issue from this adulterous union being twin boys, Sherlock and a vampire brother. Moreover, it is revealed that Mrs. Holmes became a vampire after death, and was later dispatched in the traditional manner by her husband, aided by his eldest son, Mycroft. To devotees of the original Sherlock Holmes stories the foregoing is tantamount to blasphemy, but admirers of Stoker's masterpiece will be equally shocked to find that Mina Harker has become Dracula's lover, and Dr. Seward, formerly a paragon of virtue, has changed into a black-hearted villain.

The other novels in the series place the "New Dracula" in contemporary settings, and appropriately shift the locale to the New World. In *An Old Friend of the Family* (1979) the Count is lured to the United States by a villainous vampiress named Morgan, who wants to eliminate him because of his restraining influence on other members of the vampire community. In the next novel, *Thorn* (1980), Dracula (posing as someone called Thorn) gets involved in a complicated plot to steal a painting by Leonardo da Vinci. The priceless work of art is a portrait of Vlad Dracula's unfaithful wife, Helen; and in flashback sequences, which switch from modern America to Renaissance Italy, we learn of the strange circumstances surrounding the couple's stormy marriage. The final volume in this increasingly preposterous series, *Dominion* (1982), is a muddled time travel adventure in which Dracula (alias Mr. Talisman) is pitted against Nimue, the Lady of the Lake. With world domination as the prize, both protagonists strive for possession of King Arthur's magic sword: Nimue is aided by demon-worshippers and lycanthropes; Dracula has Merlin on his side.

There are similar trials of strength in other contemporary Dracula novels. A titanic confrontation between Mary Shelley's indestructible man-made monster and Bram Stoker's arch-villain occurs in *Frankenstein Meets Dracula* (1977) by Don Glut; and a memorable meeting with another of fiction's immortals is arranged in *Sherlock Holmes vs. Dracula* (1978) by Loren D. Estleman. A more orthodox "Dracula" novel, Victor Samuels' *The Vampire Women* (1973), dispenses with any such gimmicks. Deriving its plot from passages in Stoker's novel, it concerns the Count's seduction of two young Englishwomen who come to stay at Castle Dracula. Even more derivative is Gerald Savory's *Count Dracula* (1977), which parallels Stoker's novel down to the smallest detail.

Further adventures of the sanguinary count and his minions have been chronicled in *Count Dracula's Canadian Affair* (1960) by Otto Fredrick, *Dracutwig* (1969) by Mallory T. Knight, *The Hardy Boys and Nancy Drew Meet Dracula* (1978) by Glen A. Larson and Michael Sloan, *Dracula's Cat* (1978) by Jan Wahl, *Dracula, Go Home* (1979) by Kim Platt, *Dracula in Love* (1979) by John Shirley, and *Dracula's Diary* (1982) by Michael Geare and Michael Corby. Short stories about horror fiction's most popular character include Woody Allen's "Count Dracula" (*Getting Even*, 1971), Jeanne Youngson's "Count Dracula and the Unicorn" (*Count Dracula and the Unicorn*, 1978), and Peter Tremayne's "Dracula's Chair" (*The Count Dracula Fan Club Book of Vampire Stories*, 1980).

Dracula's real-life counterpart, Vlad Tepes, is the unlikely hero of Asa Drake's *Crimson Kisses* (1981), a romantic episode from the warlord's youth describing how a gypsy enchantress initiated him into vampirism. The same character is cast in his more familiar role of villain in Maria Valdemi's *The Demon Lover* (1981), in which a handsome Russian prince is unwillingly turned into a vampire after coming under Vlad's evil influence. Doomed thereafter to a life of degradation, the reluctant vampire contrives to minimize the harm and suffering he must cause by selecting his victims from among the dregs of humanity. Inevitably, as befits a sentimental romance of this kind, the prince finds salvation through the love of a good woman.

Dracula's position as the most potent literary myth of the twentieth century has also made him a popular subject for poetry and lyrical verse. Recent examples include "Dracula" by Steve Kowit (*Wormwood Review 14*, No. 3, 1974); "Dracula" by L. L. Zeiger (*Kayak*, No. 40, November 1975); "Dracula and He" by Sanford Weiss (*Kayak*, No. 41, February 1976); "Dracula's Bolero" by Peter Fiore (*American Poetry Review 7*, No. 4, July/August 1978); "Dracula's Deserted Lady" by Lola Haskins (*Nimrod 26*, No. 1, Fall/Winter 1982); "Three Songs from *Dracula*: A Threnody of Wolves, Renfield's Litany, The Bloofer Lady" by Michael R. Collings (*Space & Time*, Summer 1983); and "Dracula's Wives" by Regina Barreca (*Women's Review of Books 1*, No. 3, December 1983).

Two excellent annotated editions of Bram Stoker's *magnum opus* have also been published. The earlier of the two versions, *The Annotated Dracula* (1976), edited by Leonard Wolf, is an exact reproduction of the text of the first edition of 1897, containing masses of associated material, including maps, drawings, photographs, and a bibliography. The second version, *The Essential Dracula* (1979), edited by Raymond T. McNally and Radu Florescu, differs in one major respect from its predecessor in that it has references to Stoker's original notes, whose existence was previously unknown to Dracula scholars, and which the editors discovered, by chance, at the Rosenbach Foundation archives in Philadelphia,

Vampire Series

Apart from the various Dracula novels and those about Barnabas Collins and his gang, several other series of novels have had a vampire as the central character. Foremost among these are Chelsea Quinn Yarbro's historical novels about a romantic vampire-hero called the Count de Saint-Germain. Fabulously wealthy, yet intensely lonely, he spends most of his time roaming around the world in search of love and understanding; and his good looks and courtly manners ensure that he has little difficulty in finding beautiful women who are willing to donate small quantities of their blood in return for a night of passionate lovemaking. Although this may make him sound like an amalgam of the Count of Monte Christo, Casanova, and Dracula, the character is, in fact, loosely based on a mysterious 18th-century alchemist of the same name who was rumored to have discovered the secret of immortality. Like Dracula, Ms. Yarbro's vampire-count is not totally invulnerable; for although he has managed to survive hundreds of years beyond the normal life span—never aging or changing physically—his existence can still be terminated in a variety of ways: by burning, decapitation, severance of the spinal column, or long exposure to sunlight or water without the protection of his native soil, which he constantly carries about his person in specially constructed shoes.

Written in a lush, romantic style, the series is comprised of five novels, each set in a different period of history. The inaugural volume, *Hotel Transylvania* (1978), takes place in Paris in 1744, and involves the Count's attempts to rescue his lover from the clutches of a group of Satanists; the second, *The Palace* (1978), recreates those turbulent days in Renaissance Florence when Savonarola held the city in the grip of religious hysteria; and, going even further back in time, the third, *Blood Games* (1979), depicts the brutality of first-century Rome during the bloody reign of Nero. Generally, in these three novels, Saint-Germain remains aloof from the historical events going on around him, preferring to offer comfort and compassion to a bevy of damsels in distress; but in the fourth volume in the series, *Path of the Eclipse* (1981), he temporarily forsakes the boudoir for the battlefield, on which he encounters the hordes of Genghis Khan. However, in the fifth and final adventure, *Tempting Fate* (1982), the usual formula is restored, with the Count coming to the rescue of an ill-fated young lady who is being persecuted by the Nazis.

A collection of short stories featuring the amorous count was published in 1983. Titled *The Saint-Germain Chronicles*, it contains "Spider Glass," "Cabin 33," "Art Songs," "Seat Partner," and "Renewal." Also included is an essay explaining the genesis of the protagonist.

Similarly noted for the authenticity of their historical backgrounds are Les Daniels' novels about the undead Spanish nobleman, Don Sebastian de Villanueva. Almost the exact opposite of Yarbro's hero, Sebastian is a cold-hearted villain who becomes increasingly hostile and bitter as the series progresses. *The Black Castle* (1978), which introduced this offbeat character, is set in 16th-century Spain at the height of the Inquisition, and revolves around an unholy pact between Sebastian and his elder brother, Diego. The latter, a power-hungry Grand Inquisitor, agrees to supply his vampiric sibling with victims from among the inmates of the papal dungeons in return for the recipient's promise to ghost-write for him the definitive book on witchcraft. In the event, however, their scheme is a total disaster, setting in motion a chain of events which culminate in the downfall of the evil duo. Diego gets his just deserts when he is staked to death after being turned into a vampire against his will, and Sebastian seemingly ends his own unnatural existence by setting fire to himself.

In the equally gloomy sequel, *The Silver Skull* (1979), Sebastian is resurrected from the dead after his skull is transported to the New World by an unscrupulous alchemist. Much of the action which follows is set against Cortez' assault on the Aztec capital, Tenochtitlan, in 1521. The third volume, *Citizen Vampire* (1981), has the French Revolution as a backdrop. Once again the indestructible Spaniard is pitted against adversaries hardly less evil than himself, including such historical luminaries as Dr. Guillotine and the Marquis de Sade.

Vampirism of a more perverse kind rears its head in the controversial Sime/Gen novels co-authored by Jean Lorrah and Jacqueline Lichtenberg. Heavy with sado-masochistic overtones, they are set in the far future when humanity has mutated into two races: the subordinate Gens, who generate a life-giving fluid called Selyn, and the dominant Simes, who need this vital substance to survive. The series commenced in 1980 with *First Channel*, and subsequent titles have included *House of Zeor*, *Unto Zeor Forever*, *Zelerod's Doom*, and *Channel's Destiny*.

Tailor-made for pimply adolescents, but a big yawn for more mature readers, are Ron Goulart's mildly titillating "Vampirella" novels featuring a voluptuous extraterrestrial vampiress. The six-volume series is comprised of *Bloodstalk* (1975), *On Alien Wings* (1975), *Deadwalk* (1976), *Blood Wedding* (1976), *Deathgame* (1976), and *Snakegod* (1976).

Equally banal are J. N. Williamson's potboilers about a lovely Greek vampiress called Lamia Zacharius, who drives her victims to their doom in her death-coach. The four novels making up the series are *Death-Coach* (1981), *Death-Angel* (1981), *Death-School* (1982), and *Death-Doctor* (1982).

Blockbusters

At the height of the horror fiction boom in the seventies two very different vampire novels succeeded in making the bestseller lists. One was Stephen King's *'Salem's Lot* (1975); the other was Anne Rice's *Interview with the Vampire* (1976). Both have subsequently acquired the status of cult classics, guaranteeing them a place on most horror fans short-list of favorite novels.

'Salem's Lot, which is intentionally patterned on Stoker's *Dracula*, yet has touches of the gory, no-holds-barred horror of the fifties horror comics, is certainly not for those of a nervous disposition. Contemporary in setting, it concerns a vampire epidemic in a small New England town, and follows the efforts made by a handful of townspeople to combat the growing horror in their midst. Their leader, a writer named Ben Mears, discovers that the source of the contagion is a modern-day counterpart of Count Dracula, who has established his headquarters in a deserted house on the edge of town. Calling himself Barlow, he makes an invincible adversary during the hours of darkness, gradually whittling his opponents down to two in number: Mears and an eleven-year-old boy. But, although the odds are stacked against them, it is Mears and his young companion who are ultimately triumphant; for despite being powerless to prevent the rest of the community becoming vampires, they still have the grim satisfaction of destroying the master-vampire after a harrowing confrontation in his lair.

Over four hundred pages long, and written in a crisp, uncluttered style, *'Salem's Lot* retains the reader's credulity throughout by making the sequence of events totally believable, no matter how bizarre they ultimately become. Constructed like a typical Hitchcock movie, the long, attenuated exposition proceeds at a leisurely pace as the atmosphere is built up, leading to the abrupt intervention of the supernatural halfway into the story. In contrast, the second half of the novel is horror undiluted, increasing in intensity as the unforgettable climax approaches.

More literary than King's blockbuster, Anne Rice's *Interview with the Vampire* was not only an instant hit with horror fans, but was also lavishly praised by the critics. One called it "the most seductive evocation of evil ever written;" another wrote that "it must stand alongside Bram Stoker's *Dracula*." Using the framing device of a tape-recorded interview, the story is narrated by a sympathetic vampire named Louis, whose age is perpetually frozen at twenty-five. Not one of the Undead by choice, he was forcibly initiated into the cult in 1791 by a vampire named Lestat. At first Louis resisted the change in himself, but eventually had to succumb to the vampire's compulsive thirst for blood, killing for it without remorse. Rejecting Lestat's company—for whom he feels only loathing—Louis forms a close relationship with one of his own victims, a five-year-old girl named Claudia, who accompanies him on his travels across Europe in search of others of his kind. The long, eventful search finally ends in Paris, where contact is made with a community of existential vampires.

Generally morbid and depressing in tone, this novel's unique fascination lies in the way it minutely examines the vampire's innermost feelings, transforming a somewhat pedestrian plot into a *tour de force*. The long-awaited sequel, *The Vampire Lestat,* finally surfaced in 1985. As the title implies, the spotlight falls upon the first novel's dark villain, and concerns his quest to find his roots, which he eventually traces back to the Adam and Eve of vampires—"They Who Must Be Kept." However, Lestat's plans to release his findings to the world, via his autobiography and a rock album, causes conflict with his fellow vampires, who fear his revelations will upset the delicate balance which exists between the world of mortals and vampires.

With readers demanding more realism in their horror fiction nowadays, a number of writers have attempted to update the vampire myth, making the vampires in their novels more believable by stripping them of most of the supernatural attributes with which they were formerly associated. The novel which pioneered this new, sophisticated image of the vampire was *The Vampire Tapestry* (1980), by the leading feminist writer Suzy McKee Charnas. Her central character is Edward Lewis Weyland, a highly intelligent vampire who has lived the equivalent of several human lifetimes. Recently awakened from a self-imposed period of hibernation lasting fifty years, he is masquerading as a professor of anthropology at a college in upstate New York. This assumed guise has been carefully chosen as the one best suited to enable him to rapidly adapt to the cultural, social, and technological changes that have occurred in his absence; but his cover is blown when a cleaning woman at the college finds out what he really is and shoots him. Although severely wounded, Weyland manages to make good his escape, and is picked up by a group of curiosity-seekers, who feed him on blood stolen from a local blood-bank until he is fully recovered. The rest of the episodic narrative describes Weyland's adventures in the hostile environment of the big city. Along the way he is held prisoner by a Satanist, voluntarily undergoes psychological therapy, and commits murder. One hesitates to wholeheartedly agree with the critic who enthusiastically declared that it was "possibly the outstanding vampire novel of all time," but there can be no doubt that the publication of *The Vampire Tapestry* marked a turning point in the development of the vampire story.

Another author who has redefined the vampire myth in the context of a contemporary setting is Whitley Strieber. In one of the best horror novels of the modern era, *The Hunger* (1981), he hypothesizes that vampires are members of a parallel race, physically like human beings but constitutionally quite different. Dominating the novel is the lamia-like Miriam Blaylock, one of the most awesome female vampires in all of fiction. Thousands of years old, yet ravishingly beautiful, she seeks a new companion to share eternity with her, and embarks on the seduction of an attractive young woman involved in scientific research into immortality. To achieve her objective, Miriam allows herself to be studied at the medical center where the woman works, knowing that her superhuman strength and vastly superior intellect will enable her to avoid incarceration should the investigations eventually expose her true nature. Sparsely plotted though it is, this well-crafted novel builds up to a tremendous climax, the author cleverly eschewing the customary "happy ending" for one that is guaranteed to shock even the most hardened horror fan.

The "parallel-race" theory has also been exploited to good effect in Ray Garton's *Seductions* (1985), a suspenseful sex-horror novel about demonic vampires. No name is given to these non-human predators, but it is suggested that they are an ancient race that inhabit underground tunnels, periodically emerging from their lairs when hunger drives them to the surface to feed. Similar to the succuba-demons of medieval folklore, they are able to adopt human form, appearing before their intended victims in the guise of their ideal lover. In order to feed, the demon must first seduce the person it has chosen, and when both have reached the height of their passion during sexual intercourse, snapping teeth emerge from the demon's genitals and devour the unsuspecting victim in a matter of seconds, leaving only a pool of blood behind.

An old-fashioned thriller which achieved success without recourse to sexual titillation or gratuitous violence was *The Keep* (1981), by F. Paul Wilson. Set during the early part of the Second World War, all the action centers round a medieval fortress overlooking the Dinu Pass, high in the Transylvanian Alps. The horror begins when a detachment of German soldiers stationed at the lonely outpost are brutally killed, one at a time, by an unknown assassin. At length it is revealed that the perpetrator of these gruesome murders is an immortal vampire named Rasalom, who has been a prisoner inside the keep since the fifteenth century, held there by the power of a talisman buried deep within the walls. Desperate to escape so that he can wreak havoc in the war-torn world outside, Rasalom has been turning the dead soldiers into zombies, and deploying them to search for the magical artifact in the cellars of the castle. The only one powerful enough to put a stop to his fiendish machinations is Glaeken. Like Rasalom, he too is an immortal being who was born many thousands of years ago in The First Age, when the forces of Light and Chaos vied for supremacy over the world. Ever since, Glaeken and Rasalom have been on opposite sides, neither one able to defeat the other. But, with Rasalom on the verge of making a successful bid for freedom, Glaeken realizes that he must finally slay his deadly foe, or the world will come under his evil domination.

A battle between Good and Evil is also the basis for George R. R. Martin's bestselling vampire novel *Fevre Dream* (1982), which is set on the Mississippi river during the colorful steamboat era. At the beginning of the story, Abner Marsh, a steamboat captain down on his luck, is approached by Joshua York, an aristocratic young gentleman who wants to build the fastest boat on the river. After going into partnership it is not long before their magnificent new boat, *Fevre Dream*, is setting out on its maiden voyage from St. Louis to New Orleans. But Abner soon becomes alarmed by the strange behavior of his companion, who sleeps all day, drinks copiously from a bottle containing a vile liquid, takes a close interest in newspaper reports of unsolved murders along the Mississippi, and makes lengthy and unexplained trips ashore. Eventually Abner learns that Joshua is using the steamboat's voyage to seek out his deadly enemy, Damon Julian, the master of the last enclave of an ancient race of vampires descended from Cain. Following his exposure, Joshua, a "cured" vampire, offers his captain a stark choice: either help him destroy the vampire-master, or flee for his life.

Feasts of Blood

Trying to trace the original source of some of the rarer stories mentioned within these pages can be a lengthy and costly business, so for the reader whose time and money are at a premium the most accessible storehouse of vampire stories are the score or more vampire anthologies which have appeared at regular intervals since the early 1960s.

The first anthology devoted exclusively to the vampire story was *The Vampire*, edited by Ornella Volta and Valeria Riva. Originally published in Italy in 1960, it was subsequently adapted into English by Margaret Crosland and published in England in 1963 under the Neville

Spearman imprint. A well-balanced selection, with 19th-century and modern authors equally represented, it also contains an extract from Calmet's much-plundered dissertation *The Phantom World*; and has a foreword by the celebrated French film director, Roger Vadim. Least-known of the thirteen stories are "Carnival" by Lawrence Durrell, "Chriseis" by Simon Raven (an extract from his novel *Doctors Wear Scarlet*), and the "post-holocaust" black comedy "Fresh Guy" by E. C. Tubb. For purely commercial reasons, one suspects, the English version of this anthology differs greatly from the original Italian edition, which contained extra non-fiction items, including essays by Voltaire and Pope Benedict XIV. With their excision the page count has been drastically reduced from a massive 787 to a modest 286 pages.

The first paperback anthology of vampire stories was *A Feast of Blood* (Avon Books, 1967), in which the editor, Charles M. Collins, served up a mouth-watering repast. The main course is made up of established favorites, such as "The Mysterious Stranger" and "Wake Not the Dead;" but among the rarer delicacies are Richard Matheson's "Blood Son" and D. Scott-Moncrieff's "Schloss Wappenburg."

Similarly, the prolific British anthologist, Peter Haining, catered for a variety of tastes in *The Midnight People* (Leslie Frewin, 1968). Inevitably, there are the usual "old chestnuts" on the menu—including extracts from those two old warhorses, *Varney the Vampire* and *Dracula*—but one is also offered the chance to sample more exotic fare with the inclusion of E. F. Benson's "And No Bird Sings," Manly Wade Wellman's "When it was Moonlight," and P. Schuyler Miller's "Over the River." The only unpalatable piece among the generous helping of eighteen stories is Basil Copper's "Dr. Porthos," which was specially commissioned by the editor. Its downfall is the surprise ending, at which point the narrator is revealed as the vampire, and describes himself being put to death by staking. To me, this conjures up the ludicrous spectacle of the storyteller feverishly working on his blood-spattered manuscript while his assailant hammers the stake into his heart. This, surely, is taking artistic license a little too far.

In 1971, as a follow-up to their earlier success, Neville Spearman published a second volume of vampire stories titled *The Undead*. Edited by James Dickie, its erudite and highly literate introduction is echoed in the choice of stories, each penned by a master of his craft. Supplementing the obligatory classics are a handful of imaginative gems from the pages of *Weird Tales*, namely H. P. Lovecraft's "The Hound,"

Everil Worrell's "The Canal," Carl Jacobi's "Revelations in Black," and two by the great C. A. Smith, "The End of the Story" and "The Death of Ilalotha."

A minor anthology from the same period is Margaret Carter's *The Curse of the Undead* (Fawcett Gold Medal Books, 1970). Not a particularly original selection, the only stories not readily available elsewhere are Niel Straum's "Vanishing Breed" and Evelyn E. Smith's "Softly While You're Sleeping." A more even balance between vintage and modern stories is struck in *Dracula's Guest and Other Stories* (1972), a little-known anthology compiled by Vic Ghidalia for the Xerox Company. As well as the title story, it contains F. Marion Crawford's "For the Blood is the Life," Marion Brandon's "The Dark Castle," Robert Bloch's "The Cloak," August Derleth's "Bat's Belfry," and Joseph Payne Brennan's "The Hunt."

Two anthologies from the mid-seventies which mix short stories with factual accounts of vampirism culled from old treatises are *A Clutch of Vampires* (New York Graphic Society, 1974), edited by Raymond T. McNally, and *Vampires of the Slavs* (Slavica Publishers, 1976), edited by Jan L. Perkowski.

Disappointingly predictable in its choice of stories is *The Dracula Book of Great Vampire Stories* (Citadel Press, 1977), edited by Leslie Shepard. Once again the same tired old classics are reprinted, and the few rarities that have been included, such as Victor Rowan's "Four Wooden Stakes" and Mary Braddon's "Good Lady Ducayne," hardly deserve to be called great. A more adventurous selection of stories can be found in another anthology published in 1977, *The Rivals of Dracula* (Corgi Books), edited by Michel Parry. Great Value, it includes "The Vampire of Kaldenstein" by Frederick Cowles, "The Guardian of the Cemetery" by Jean Ray, "The Story of Baelbrow" by E. & H. Heron, "The Undead Die" by E. Everett Evans, "The Horror Undying" by Manly Wade Wellman, "The Bat is My Brother" by Robert Bloch, "Blood Brother" by Charles Beaumont, "Something Had to be Done" by David Drake, "Night Life" by Steven Utley, and "Conversion" by Ramsey Campbell.

More intellectual in its appeal is *The Vampyre: Lord Ruthven to Count Dracula* (Gollancz, 1978). Edited by Christopher Frayling, a university lecturer, it contains extracts describing the most influential vampires of folklore, essays on the sexual bases of the myth, and an assortment of short stories dating from what the editor describes as "the

most creative period in the development of the Vampire Count and the
Fatal Woman as figures in European fantasy literature—between Lord
Byron and Bram Stoker." The authors featured include Alexandre Dumas,
E. T. A. Hoffmann, Alexis Tolstoy, Fitz-James O'Brien, and Julian
Osgood Field (alias 'X. L.'). Aimed primarily at the academically-minded,
the book also has a long, fastidiously researched introduction, which
traces the development of the vampire theme in 19th-century literature.

Classic stories also predominate in *The Count Dracula Fan Club
Book of Vampire Stories* (1980) and *The Count Dracula Book of Classic
Vampire Tales* (1981), both edited by Jeanne Youngson. Two stories
original to the latter are "Dracula's Chair" by Peter Tremayne and "The
S.O.B.: A Vampire Western" by Jeanne Youngson.

After a few blank years, the next all-vampire anthology to appear
was *Vampire: Chilling Tales of the Undead* (Target Books, 1985), edited
by Peter Haining. Always one for giving his customers value for money,
Haining has dipped into the pages of old fantasy magazines for his
selection of fifteen stories, many of which will be unknown even to the
most avid fan. Resurrected after many years out of print are Frank Owen's
"The Tinkle of the Camel's Bell," James Hart's "The Traitor," Robert
Thurston Hopkins' "The Vampire of Woolpit Grange," Curt Siodmak's
"Experiment with Evil," Phil Robinson's "The Last of the Vampires,"
and Edith Wharton's "Bewitched."

Stories from old magazines are also strongly represented in *Vamps*
(DAW, 1987), in which the editors, Martin H. Greenberg and Charles
G. Waugh, have assembled sixteen works of fiction featuring female
vampires. Proving that the female of the species really is deadlier than
the male are Stephen King's "One for the Road," William Tenn's "She
Only Goes Out at Night," Théophile Gautier's "Clarimonda," Robert
Bloch's "The Cloak," F. Marion Crawford's "For the Blood is the Life,"
Manly Wade Wellman's "The Last Grave of Lill Warran" and "When
it was Moonlight," Fritz Leiber's "The Girl with the Hungry Eyes,"
Julian Hawthorne's "Ken's Mystery," Seabury Quinn's "Restless Souls,"
August Derleth's "The Drifting Snow," Mary E. Wilkins-Freeman's
"Luella Miller," Richard Matheson's "Dress of White Silk," Tanith Lee's
"Red as Blood," and J. Sheridan Le Fanu's "Carmilla."

One of the most impressive collections of vampire stories to appear
in recent years is *Dracula's Brood* (The Aquarian Press, 1987). In what
was obviously a labor of love, the editor, Richard Dalby, has gathered
together no less than twenty-three rare vampire stories written by friends

and contemporaries of Bram Stoker. Familiar classics have been deliberately avoided in favor of neglected works hitherto buried in old books, or lost in the pages of long-forgotten magazines. Receiving their first publication for many years are William Gilbert's "The Last Lords of Gardonal," Phil Robinson's "The Man-Eating Tree," Vincent O'Sullivan's "Will," H. B. Marriott-Watson's "The Stone Chamber," Hume Nisbet's "The Vampire Maid" and "The Old Portrait," Vernon Lee's "Marsyas in Flanders," Louise J. Strong's "An Unscientific Story," Sabine Baring-Gould's "A Dead Finger," Horacio Quiroga's "The Feather Pillow," Alice and Claude Askew's "Aylmer Vance and the Vampire," Ulric Daubeny's "The Sumach," M. R. James' "The Wailing Well," E. Heron-Allen's "Another Squaw?," and E. R. Punshon's "The Living Stone." Neglected works by some of the most distinguished names in weird fiction have also been revived. A notable find made by Dalby is Algernon Blackwood's "The Singular Death of Morton," which appears in print for the first time since its original publication in the December 1910 issue of *The Tramp* magazine. Even rarer is "Princess of Darkness," a hitherto unpublished story by Frederick Cowles.

A more familiar repast is served up in *Vampires: Two Centuries of Great Vampire Stories* (Doubleday, 1987), edited by Alan Ryan. Making up the contents of this mammoth anthology are Lord Byron's "Fragment of a Novel," an excerpt from James Malcolm Rymer's *Varney the Vampyre*, the anonymously-written "The Mysterious Stranger," J. Sheridan Le Fanu's "Carmilla," Mary Elizabeth Braddon's "Good Lady Ducayne," Bram Stoker's "Dracula's Guest," Mary E. Wilkins-Freeman's "Luella Miller," F. Marion Crawford's "For the Blood is the Life," Algernon Blackwood's "The Transfer," E. F. Benson's "The Room in the Tower," M. R. James' "An Episode of Cathedral History," Clark Ashton Smith's "A Rendezvous in Averoigne," C. L. Moore's "Shambleau," Carl Jacobi's "Revelations in Black," Manly Wade Wellman's "School for the Unspeakable," August Derleth's "The Drifting Snow," P. Schuyler Miller's "Over the River," Fritz Leiber's "The Girl with the Hungry Eyes," C. M. Kornbluth's "The Mindworm," Richard Matheson's "Drink My Blood," Charles Beaumont's "Place of Meeting," Robert Bloch's "The Living Dead," Robert Aickman's "Pages from a Young Girl's Journal," R. Chetwynd-Hayes' "The Werewolf and the Vampire," Charles L. Grant's "Love-Starved," Chelsea Quinn Yarbro's "Cabin 33," Suzy McKee Charnas' "Unicorn Tapestry," Alan Ryan's "Following the Way," Ramsey Campbell's "The Sunshine Club," Steve

Rasnic Tem's "The Men & Women of Rivendale," and Tanith Lee's "Bite-Me-Not or, Fleur de Feu." Headnotes by the editor give an added interest to the stories, although the introduction and appendices expose his limited knowledge of the subject.

Anthologies which combine vampire stories with werewolf stories have also proved popular over recent years. They include *Monsters Galore!* (Fawcett Publications, 1965), edited by Bernhardt J. Hurwood; *The Dark Shadows Book of Vampires and Werewolves* (Paperback Library, 1970), edited by Hurwood but credited to Barnabas and Quentin Collins; *Monster Tales: Vampires, Werewolves, and Things* (Rand McNally, 1973), edited by Roger Elwood; *Vampires, Werewolves & Other Monsters* (Curtis, 1974), edited by Roger Elwood; and *Vampires, Werewolves and Phantoms of the Night* (Methuen, 1983), edited by Winifred Finlay.

For the insatiable vampire addict, further mouth-watering tidbits are served up in two anthologies of vampire poems published by The Count Dracula Fan Club, *The Further Perils of Dracula* (1979) and *The Vampire in Verse* (1985). The former is a collection of light verse by Jeanne Youngson, consisting of twenty-one rhymed-and-metered poems; the latter, edited by Steven Moore, is a bumper collection of vampire verse, ranging from 18th-century ballads to contemporary pieces. Arranged in chronological order, the forty-eight poems selected are "The Vampire," by Heinrich August Ossenfelder; "Lenora," by Gottfried August Bürger; "The Bride of Corinth," by Johann Wolfgang von Goethe; "Christabel," by Samuel Taylor Coleridge; "Thalaba the Destroyer," by Robert Southey; "The Vampyre," by John Stagg; "The Giaour," by Lord Byron; "La Belle Dame sans Merci" and "Lamia," by John Keats; "The Vampire Bride," by Henry Liddell; "Clarimonde," by Théophile Gautier, "The Vampyre," by James Clerk Maxwell; "The Vampyre," by Vasile Alecsandri; "The Vampire" and "Metamorphoses of the Vampire," by Charles Baudelaire; "The Vampire," by Arthur Symons; "The Vampire," by Rudyard Kipling; "The Vampire," by Madison Cawein; "The Vampire," by Efrén Rebolledo; "La Belle Morte," by Conrad Aiken; "The Vampires Won't Vampire for Me," by F. Scott Fitzgerald; "Enter the Vampire," by Clement Wood; "Stephen's Vampire Poem," by James Joyce; "The Vampire: 1914," by Conrad Aiken; "Vampire," by Bertrande Harry Snell; "Oil and Blood," by William Butler Yeats; "The Vampire," by Herbert E. Palmer; "Vampire Bride," by Felix Stefanile; "Vampire," by Walter H. Kerr; "The Vampire," by David Galler; "The Vampire Housewife," by Ruth Fainlight; "Vampire's Aubade," by W. D.

Snodgrass; "The Vampire's Tryst" and "The Onlooker," by Wade Wellman; "Voices Answering Back: The Vampires" and "Vampires," by Lawrence Raab; "To His Mistress, Dead and Darkly Return'd," by Roger Johnson; "The Vampire," by John DeWitt; "Vampire," by Ray Amorosi; "The Vampire" by Gregory Orr; "Dracula" by Steve Kowit; "Vampire," by Jean Pedrick; "Why Don't They Go Back to Transylvania?," by Robert Peters; "Vampyr," by Stephen Spera; "A Vampyre Legend" and "Revenant," by Kathleen Resch; "The Vampire's Love Song," by Margaret G. Keyes and Jeanne Youngson; "Jazz Vamp," by Maurice Cloud; "Dominatrix," by Clifford Young; and "The Blood Countess," by Robert Peters.

Clearly the number of vampire anthologies published in the 1980s indicates that the public's interest in vampire stories is as great as it ever was, encouraging me to hope that this survey will provide anthologists with plenty of ideas for further selections.

Addendum

Included in this supplementary list are novels and short stories that were overlooked in the main body of the survey, along with some recent additions to the vampire canon.

NOVELS

The Three Coffins, by John Dickson Carr (Harper & Brothers, New York, 1935; rpt. Dell, New York, 1965).

Vampires of Venus, by Karl Mannheim (Pemberton, Manchester, 1950).

Blood Money, by Jack Lewis (Headline Books, Los Angeles, 1960).

He Who Whispers, by John Dickson Carr (Bantam Books, New York, 1965).

The Adult Version of Dracula, by Hal Kantor (Calga Publishers, Los Angeles, 1970).

One More Time, by Michael Avallone (Popular Library, New York, 1970).

Blood Moon, by Jean Alexander (Lancer Books, New York, 1970).

Brother Blood, by Peter Saxon (Belmont Books, New York, 1970).

Vampire's Moon, by Peter Saxon (Belmont Books, New York, 1970).

The Vampires of Finistere, by Peter Saxon (Berkley Books, New York, 1970).

The Vampire of Moura, by Virginia Coffman (Ace Books, New York 1970).

The Other People, by Pat A. Briscoe (Powell, Reseda, 1970).

The Thing, by J. J. Madison (Belmont Tower Books, New York, 1971).

The Curse of the Concullens, by Florence Stevenson (New American Library, New York 1972). A modern Gothic novel in which the heroine encounters just about every occult manifestation imaginable, including banshees, werewolves, and the local vampire—an Irish patriot who bites only British soldiers.

The Vampires, by John Rechy (Grove Press, New York, 1973).

Bloodsport, by Robert F. Jones (Simon & Schuster, New York, 1974).

The Vampires and the Witch, by Lee Falk (Avon Books, New York, 1974).

Children of the Night, by Richard Lortz (Dell, New York, 1974).

The Vampire Contessa: From the Journal of Jeremy Quentain, by Marilyn Ross (Pinnacle, New York, 1974).

Vampire in the Shadows, by Marc Lovell (Doubleday, New York, 1974). Also known by the alternative title of *An Enquiry into the Existence of Vampires*, leading certain bibliographers to mistakenly classify it as a non-fiction book.

The Vampire of Mons, by Desmond Stewart (Harper & Row, New York, 1976). Two boys at a run-down boarding school dabble in the occult and vampirism after becoming involved with their eccentric schoolmaster.

Sandworld, by Richard A. Lupoff (Berkley Medallion, New York, 1976). Science fiction novel in which the crew of a space-ship are stranded on a planet populated by a race of vampires.

Nightwing, by Martin Cruz Smith (Norton, New York, 1977). Describes the mounting threat to human life posed by a horde of disease-ridden vampire bats.

The Virgin and the Vampire, by Robert J. Myers (Pocket Books, New York, 1977).

The Dance of Blood, by Stewart Farrar (Arrow Books, London, 1977).

The Vampire Tapes, by Arabella Randolphe (Berkley Medallion, New York, 1977).

Mind of My Mind, by Octavia Butler (Doubleday, New York, 1977).

Tabitha fffoulkes, by John Linssen (Arbor House, New York, 1978).

The Bad Sister, by Emma Tennant (Coward, McCann & Geoghegan, New York, 1978).

Bloodthirst, by Mark Ronson (Hamlyn, London, 1979).

The Glow, by Brooks Stanwood (McGraw-Hill, New York, 1979). Slow-paced novel concerning a modern-day cult of blood-drinkers.

The Vampire Chase, by Stephen Brett (Manor Books, New York, 1979).

By Blood Alone, by Bernhardt J. Hurwood (Charter Books, New York, 1979). Crime thriller with a sub-plot about a vampire named Zachery Lucius Sexton.

The Devil's Kiss, by William W. Johnstone (Zebra Books, New York, 1980).

To Love a Vampire, by Nigel Fleming (World-Wide Publishing, Encino, CA, 1980).

Never Cross a Vampire, by Stuart Kaminsky (St. Martin's Press, New York, 1980).

Kamtellar, by R. Chetwynd-Hayes. In *The Fantastic World of Kamtellar* (William Kimber, London, 1980). A parallel-world fantasy set in a land ruled by vampires.

Night Whispers, by Charles Veley (Doubleday, New York, 1980). Members of a secret cult thriving in New York City are given a combination of drugs and blood infusions in order to acquire prolonged health and youth.

The Wanting Factor, by Gene DeWeese (Playboy Paperbacks, New York, 1980). A vampire stalks a small Indiana college town, thirsting for souls.

Sabella; or The Blood Stone, by Tanith Lee (DAW Books, New York, 1980). Offbeat science fiction novel about a sensuous femme fatale who seduces young men in order to satisfy her craving for blood.

A Taste for Power, by Muriel Dobbin (Marek/Putnam, New York, 1980).

Vegas Vampire, by Jory Sherman (Pinnacle Books, Los Angeles, 1980). Features psychic investigator "Chill" Childers, who tracks down a vampire who is slowly wiping out a casino's chorus line.

The Partaker, by R. Chetwynd-Hayes (William Kimber, London, 1980). About an ancient race of vampires still surviving today. Banded together in small, scattered communities, they partake of blood like other vampires, but hold to the mandatory rule "Thou Shalt Not Drain." The novel's central character, Carlos Markland, is the first boy-cub to be born to them for two hundred years; but their joy is shortlived. Things start to go wrong when Carlos' elders are forced to send him to school, where he is bullied by the other boys. Goaded into retaliation, he commits the unpardonable sin of draining the blood of one of his tormentors, which results in the creation of an army of vampiric zombies called "The Creepers."

Vampyr, by Jan Jennings (Pinnacle Books, New York, 1981). A strange virus in the bloodstream compels a community of people to drink blood, which they take from willing donors.

Flowers of Evil, by Robert Charles (Futura, London, 1981). Concerns a threat to mankind from blood-drinking flowers.

The Nursery, by Lewis Mallory (Hamlyn, London, 1981). Another variation on the vampire-plant theme.

The Intrusion, by David Combs (Avon Books, New York, 1981).

Lamia, by Michael Gardine (Dell, New York, 1981).

Vampires of Nightworld, by David Bischoff (Ballantine/Del Rey, New York, 1981).

Ludlow's Mill, by R. R. Walters (Pinnacle, New York, 1981).

Moonlight Variations, by Florence Stevenson (Jove, New York, 1981).

Blood County, by Curt Selby (DAW Books, New York, 1981). An isolated West Virginian mountain community is ruled over by a self-styled vampire.

They Thirst, by Robert R. McCammon (Avon Books, New York, 1981). Spectacular, but crudely written blockbuster, in which Los Angeles is menaced by a 400-year-old vampire masquerading as a teenaged hoodlum. The ending, where Los Angeles sinks into the ocean, it totally ludicrous.

Warhead, by Guy N. Smith (New English Library, London, 1981). Violent shocker in which vampires attack a British missile base.

Cry Vampire!, by Terrance Dicks (Blackie, Glasgow, 1981).

Bloodshift, by Garfield Reeves-Stevens (Virgo Paperbacks, Toronto, 1981).

Blood Will Have Blood, by Linda J. Barnes (Avon Books, New York, 1982). The backdrop to this mystery novel is a stage production of *Dracula*.

Miranda, by Edlyne Bond (Phantom Press, Lawndale, CA, 1982).

The Delicate Dependency: A Novel of the Vampire Life, by Michael Talbot (Avon Books, New York, 1982). A romantic horror novel set in the Victorian era, which portrays vampires as highly intellectual beings who spend their extra-long lives advancing their knowledge and trying to save the human race from destroying itself.

The Reluctant Vampire, by Eric Morecambe (Methuen, London, 1982). A comic novel primarily intended for young readers. Full of wit and wordplay, it tells of the "goings on" in the small village of Katchem-by-the-throat in the tiny country of Gotcha. A sequel, *The Vampire's Revenge*, was published in 1984.

The Blood Monsters, by Guy N. Smith (New English Library, London, 1982).

Castle Dubrava, by Yuri Kapralov (Dutton, New York, 1982).

The Ice Maiden, by Marc Behm. In *Three Novels* (Zomba Books, London, 1982).

Dhampire, by Scott Baker (Pocket Books/Timescape, New York, 1982).

The Initiation, by Robert Brunn (Dell, New York, 1982).

Curse of the Vampire, by Karl Alexander (Pinnacle Books, New York, 1982).

New Blood, by Richard Salem (Tor Books, New York, 1982). Two young married couples who flee the rigors of city life for the seemingly idyllic town of Credence, West Virginia, discover that the town *literally* thrives on new blood.

The Darkangel, by Meredith Ann Pierce (Atlantic-Little, Brown, New York, 1982). A highly acclaimed fantasy novel set in the far future when the Moon has been given an atmosphere and is inhabited by specially adapted people and a variety of fabulous creatures. The villain of the piece is a vampire whose power increases with each new soul he steals.

The Undead, by Guy N. Smith (New English Library, London, 1983).

Nightchild, by Scott Baker (Pocket Books/Timescape SF, New York, 1983).

The Selkie, by Charles Sheffield and David Bischoff (New American Library/Signet, New York, 1983).

The Journal of Edwin Underhill, by Peter Tonkin (Coronet, London, 1983). Haunting novel describing the gradual transformation of the hero into a vampire.

The Soft Whisper of the Dead by Charles L. Grant (Donald M. Grant, West Kingston, R. I., 1983). The setting for this novel is the imaginary New England town of Oxrun Station, during the late Victorian era. The plot concerns a vampiric nobleman's attempt to subjugate the town's populace by hypnotism.

The Awakening, by John Russo (Pocket Books, New York, 1983). Sympathetic vampire, Benjamin Latham, is unexpectedly catapulted into the twentieth century after having been unjustly executed for sorcery two hundred years earlier. Basically decent, he is appalled by the violent crime and lax moral standards of today, and sets about ridding society of some of its worst elements.

The Fellowship, by Aden and Mary Romine (Leisure Books, New York, 1984).

Blood Sport, by R. C. Scott (Bantam, New York, 1984).

I, Vampire, by Jody Scott (Ace Books, New York, 1984). A madcap romp featuring an aging female vampire called Sterling O'Blivion, who falls in love with a creature from outer space who is animating a body with a remarkable semblance to Virginia Woolf.

The Spy Who Drank My Blood, by Gordon Linzer (Space & Time, New York, 1984). Espionage thriller featuring a vampire detective.

Vampire Junction, by S. P. Somtow (The Donning Company, New York, 1984).

The Devil's Touch, by William W. Johnstone (Zebra Books, New York, 1984).

Lamia, by Tristan Travis (W. H. Allen, London, 1984).

Yellow Pages, by John Linssen (Arbor House, New York, 1985).

Blood Autumn, by Kathryn Ptacek (Tor Books, New York, 1985).

The Immortal, by John Tigges (Leisure Books, New York, 1986).

You're Next!, by Nick Sharman (New English Library, London, 1986).

Yellow Fog, by Les Daniels (Donald M. Grant, West Kingston, R. I., 1986). A continuation of the Don Sebastian saga.

Necroscope, by Brian Lumley (Grafton Books, London, 1986).

Dracula is a Pain in the Neck, by Elizabeth Levy (Star Books, London, 1986).

Tendrils, by Simon Ian Childer (Grafton Books, London, 1986). After it is released from its cocoon deep beneath the earth, a 65 million-year-old alien monster uses its myriad tentacles to penetrate the flesh of its human victims and suck out the life-force, leaving them an empty husk.

The Light at the End, by John Skipp and Craig Spector (Bantam, New York, 1986). An extremely violent novel about a teenaged vampire who brings mayhem and carnage to the New York subway.

Perfume, by Patrick Suskind (Alfred Knopf, New York, 1987). About an olfactory vampire who kills people to steal their scents.

Blood Hunt, by Lee Killough (Tor Books, New York, 1987). A detective stalks a female vampire through the back alleys of San Francisco.

The Lost Boys, by Craig Shaw Gardner (Berkley, New York, 1987).

The Goldcamp Vampire, by Elizabeth Scarborough (Bantam, New York, 1987).

Blood Worm, by John Halkin (Arrow Books, London, 1987). A terrified city is attacked by gigantic worms that turn pink after feasting on human blood. Accompanying them in the massacre are murderous beetles which look like exquisite jewels.

The Curse of the Obelisk, by Ron Goulart (Avon Books, New York, 1987).

Live Girls, by Ray Garton (Pocket Books, New York, 1987).

Bloodthirst, by J. M. Dillard (Pocket Books, New York, 1987).

The Devil's Cat, by William W. Johnstone (Zebra Books, New York, 1987).

The Devouring, by F. W. Armstrong (Tor Books, New York, 1987).

Lifeblood, by Lee Duigon (Pinnacle Books, New York, 1988).

Black Ambrosio, by Elizabeth Engstrom (Tor Books, New York, 1988).

Blood Links, by Lee Killough (Tor Books, New York, 1988). Sequel to *Blood Hunt*.

Those Who Hunt the Night, by Barbara Hambly (Del Rey, New York, 1988).

The Other Side, by R. Chetwynd-Hayes (Tor Books, New York, 1988).

Those of My Blood, by Jacqueline Lichtenberg (St. Martin's Press, New York, 1988).

The House of Caine, by Ken Eulo (Tor Books, New York, 1988).

Necroscope II: Wamphyr!, by Brian Lumley (Grafton Books, London, 1988).

In Silence Sealed, by Kathryn Ptacek (Tor Books, New York, 1988).

Erebus, by Shaun Hutson (Leisure Books, New York, 1988).

The Empire of Fear, by Brian Stableford (Simon & Schuster, New York, 1988).

The Queen of the Damned, by Anne Rice (Alfred Knopf, New York, 1988).

Blood Thirst, by L. A. Freed (Pinnacle Books, New York, 1989).

SHORT STORIES

"Only by Mortal Hands," by Henry W. A. Fairfield (*Ghost Stories*, October 1927).

"Offspring of Hell," by H. Thomson. In *Gruesome Cargoes*, edited by Christine Campbell Thompson (Selwyn & Blount, London, 1928).

"The Vampire Bat," by H. A. Keller and Edward T. Lowe (*New Mystery Adventures*, April 1935).

"Elder Brother," by Charles Caldwell Dobie. In *San Francisco Adventures* (Appleton, New York, 1937).

"The Immortal Soul," by Violet Van der Elst. In *The Torture Chamber and Other Stories* (The Doge Press, London, 1937).

"The Sisters," by Leonora Carrington. In *A Night with Jupiter and Other Fantastic Stories* (Vanguard Press, New York, 1945).

"Vampires Work at Night," by Shelley Smith (*Weird Story Magazine*, No. 1, 1946).

"Vampire of the Village," by G. K. Chesterton. In *Father Brown Omnibus* (Dodd, Mead & Co., New York, 1951).

"Haunt of the Vampire," by Max Chartair (*Supernatural Stories*, September 1954).

"Dead End," by Mack Reynolds (*Tales of the Frightened*, August 1957).

"Strange Alliance," by Bryce Walton (*Phantom*, June 1958).

"Valley of the Vampire," by Bron Fane (*Supernatural Stories*, December 1958).

"Lady Without Appetite," by John Gloag. In *In the Dead of Night*, edited by Michael Sissons (Canterbury, 1961).

"Sun of Dracula," by Lima da Costa (*Famous Monsters* 12, June 1961).

"Vampire Castle," by Pel Torro (*Supernatural Stories*, March 1962).

"The Vampire Sleeps," by Michael Avallone. In *Tales of the Frightened* (Belmont Books, New York, 1963).

"Vampire's Moon," by Rene Rolant (*Supernatural Stories*, May 1964).

"Transylvania, Here We Come," by Richard Benda and Henry Hamarck (*Famous Monsters* 26, 1964).

"Vania and the Vampire," by Dorothy G. Spicer. In *Thirteen Ghosts* (Coward McCann, New York, 1965).

"The Scarlet Lady," by Alistair Bevan (*SF Impulse*, August 1966).

"Vampires Ltd.," by Joseph Nesvadba. In *European Tales of Terror*, edited by J. J. Strating (Fontana, London, 1968).

"Dracula 2000," by Sathanas Rehan and Viktor Vesperto (*Famous Monsters* 55, May 1969).

"The Martian and the Vampire," by E. Everett Evans. In *Food for Demons* (Shroud Publishers, San Diego, 1971).

"Sleeping Beauty," by Terry Carr. In *New Worlds of Fantasy 3* (1971).

"The Vampire of Curitiba," by Dalton Trevisan. In *The Vampire of Curitiba and Other Stories* (Alfred Knopf, New York, 1972).

"Under the Tombstone," by Ken Bulmer. In *New Writings in Horror*, edited by David Sutton (Sphere Books, London, 1972).

"Sword in the Snow," by E. C. Tubb (*Weird Tales*, Fall 1973).

"Miscreant from Murania," by C. M. Eddy. In *Exit into Eternity* (Oxford Press, Providence, R. I., 1973).

"Trial of the Blood," by Barry N. Malzberg. In *The Berserkers*, edited by Roger Elwood (Trident Press, New York, 1974).

"The Vampires of Tempassuk," by Owen Rutter. In *Monsters, Monsters, Monsters*, edited by Helen Hoke (Franklin Watts, New York, 1975).

"Nedra at f:5.6.," by Harlan Ellison. In *No Doors, No Windows* (Pyramid Books, New York, 1975).

"Feeding Time," by David Bischoff and C. Lampton. In *The Fifty-Meter Monsters and Other Horrors* (Pocket Books, New York, 1976).

"Kid Cardula," by Jack Ritchie. In *Alfred Hitchcock's Tales to Take Your Breath Away* (Random House, New York, 1977).

"The Scallion Stone," by Basil A. Smith. In *Whispers*, edited by Stuart D. Schiff (Doubleday, New York, 1977). Features an amphibious plant-vampire.

"The Tale of the Vampires' Kingdom," by Italo Calvino. In *The Castle of Crossed Destinies* (Harcourt, New York, 1977).

"Blood Money," by Timothy O'Keefe. In *Alfred Hitchcock's Witch's Brew* (Random House, New York, 1977).

"Slaves of the Vampire Queen," by Michael Shea (*Phantasy Digest*, No. 3, 1977).

"The Dracula File," by Tim Stout. In *The Second Book of Unknown Tales of Horror*, edited by Peter Haining (Sidgwick & Jackson, London, 1978).

"Jerusalem's Lot," by Stephen King. In *Night Shift* (Doubleday, New York, 1978).

"The Shadow Vampire," by Leon Gammell (*Eldritch Tales*, October 1978).

"Blood Moon," by Thomas L. Owen (*Whispers*, October 1979).

"The Third Horseman," by Tanith Lee (*Weirdbook* 14, June 1979).

"Spareen Among the Tartars," by Susan C. Petrey (*The Magazine of Fantasy & Science Fiction*, September 1979). Features a band of vampires called the Varkela, who receive blood from willing donors in exchange for their services as shamans.

"The Vampire Man," by Percy Spurlark Parker (*Mike Shayne Mystery Magazine*, November 1980).

"He Found Her in Late Summer," by Peter Carey. In *Winter's Tales 25*, edited by Caroline Hobhouse (St. Martin's Press, New York, 1980).

"The Brood," by Ramsey Campbell. In *Dark Forces*, edited by Kirby McCauley (Viking Press, New York, 1980).

"Opening a Vein," by Bill Pronzini and Barry N. Malzberg. In *Shadows 3*, edited by C. L. Grant (Doubleday, New York, 1980).

"The Ancient Mind at Work," by Suzy McKee Charnas. In *Best Science Fiction Stories of the Year*, edited by Gardner Dozois (Dutton, New York, 1980).

"Spareen Among the Cossacks," by Susan C. Petrey (*The Magazine of Fantasy & Science Fiction*, April 1981).

"The Inheritance," by Alan Dean Foster. In *Horrors*, edited by Charles L. Grant (Playboy Paperbacks, New York, 1981).

"Kaeti's Nights," by Keith Roberts (*The Magazine of Fantasy & Science Fiction*, October 1981). Later spawned a full-length novel titled *Kaeti & Co.* (1986).

"The Vampire of Mallworld," by Somtow Sucharitkul (*Amazing SF Stories*, May 1981).

"The Opposite House," by John and Diane Brizzolara. In *Weird Tales 3*, edited by Lin Carter (Zebra Books, New York, 1981). Unusual story about a doppelganger world, parallel to our own, which sucks out the life of a small rural community.

"The Black Garden," by Carl Jacobi. In *Weird Tales 3*. A vampiress retains her youth by drinking the blood of slaughtered virgins.

"The Reluctant Vampire," by R. J. Connors (*Yankee* 45, October 1981).

"A Night on the Docks," by Freff (*Whispers*, August 1982). Downbeat story about a group of street-wise kids who capture a vampire and torture him to death.

"A Perfect Night for Vampires," by Alan Ryan (*Shayol*, Winter 1982). Poem.

"Onawa," by Alan Ryan. In *Death*, edited by Stuart D. Schiff (Playboy Paperbacks, New York, 1982). Told from the perspective of the vampire, a half-breed Red Indian girl.

"Beyond Any Measure," by Karl Edward Wagner. In *In a Lonely Place* (Warner, 1983). Superb combination of eroticism and horror, with an extremely bizarre twist in the tail.

"Vourdalak," by John Wysocki (*Weirdbook* 18, Summer 1983).

"Small Changes," by Susan C. Petrey (*The Magazine of Fantasy & Science Fiction*, February 1983).

"Spareen and Old Turk," by Susan C. Petrey (*The Magazine of Fantasy & Science Fiction*, August 1983).

"Territorial Imperative," by Walter Satterthwait (*The Magazine of Fantasy & Science Fiction*, April 1983).

"Peppermint Kisses," by Jesse Oburn. In *Shadows 6*, edited by Charles L. Grant (Doubleday, New York, 1983). Offbeat "post-holocaust" story in which children are the last survivors in a city haunted by the vampire-like remnants of mankind.

"The Dragons of Mons Fractus," by Richard L. Tierney (*Weirdbook* 19, Spring 1984). Set in the first century A.D., this story tells how Pontius Pilate became a vampire after Christ's crucifixion.

"Son of Celluloid," by Clive Barker. In *Books of Blood*, Volume 3 (Sphere Books, London, 1984).

"Kiss of the Lamia," by Brian Lumley (*Weirdbook* 20, Spring 1985).

"Blood Gothic," by Nancy Jones Holder. In *Shadows 8*, edited by Charles L. Grant (Doubleday, New York, 1985).

"All of You," by James V. McConnell. In *Uncollected Stars*, edited by Piers Anthony (Avon Books, New York, 1986).

"Kiss the Vampire Goodbye," by Alan Ryan. In *Quadriphobia* (Doubleday, New York, 1986).

"Vampire in the Mirror," by Gerald W. Page (*Weirdbook* 22, Summer 1987).

ANTHOLOGIES/COLLECTIONS

Tales of the Undead: Vampires and Visitants, edited by Elinore Blaisdell (Crowell, London, 1947). Only ten of the twenty-three stories have a vampire theme.

Demon Lovers and Strange Seductions, edited by Margaret L. Carter (Fawcett Gold Medal, Greenwich, CT, 1972).

Count Dracula and the Unicorn, edited by Jeanne Youngson (The Count Dracula Fan Club, New York, 1978). Contents include the title story, an extract from *Dracula*, and a vampire-film checklist.

The Best of the World of Dark Shadows, edited by Richard Robinson (Imperial Press, Dardanelle, AR, 1979).

A Child's Garden of Vampires, edited by Jeanne Youngson (The Count Dracula Fan Club, New York, 1980). Mainly a collection of vampire poetry.

Freak Show Vampire and The Hungry Grass (The Count Dracula Fan Club, New York, 1981). Contains two novellas, "Freak Show Vampire" by Jeanne Youngson, and "The Hungry Grass" by Peter Tremayne.

Vampire's Honeymoon, by Cornell Woolrich (Carroll & Graf, New York, 1985). Only the title story (better-known as "My Lips Destroy") has a vampire motif.

Dracula's Children, by R. Chetwynd-Hayes (William Kimber, London, 1987). Connected stories about individuals who have inherited Dracula's vampire mantle.

The House of Dracula, by R. Chetwynd-Hayes (William Kimber, London, 1987). More stories in the same vein.

Voices from the Vaults: Authentic Tales of Vampires and Ghosts, edited by D. P. Varma (Key Porter, Toronto, 1987). Contains mainly classic stories, including "The Tomb of Sarah," "The Room in the Tower," "For the Blood is the Life," "Count Magnus," and "The Family of the Vourdalak."

NON-FICTION

The Vampire in 19th-century English Literature, by Carol A. Senf (Bowling Green State University Popular Press, Ohio, 1988). Academic study mainly concerned with examples of metaphoric vampirism in serious literature.

Dracula: The Vampire and the Critics, edited by Margaret L. Carter (University Microfilms International, Michigan, 1988). A compilation of articles analysing Bram Stoker's novel from a variety of approaches.

Vampires, by Vincent Hillyer (Loose Change Publications, Calif., 1988). Coffee-table book with illustrations supporting the text.

Index